AF680119

AI VISUAL REFERENCE SERIES

AI Governance and Ethics Visual Reference

Andrea V.M. Greaves

© **2026 AI Awareness Limited.** All rights reserved.
"Andrea V.M. Greaves" is a pen name used by AI Awareness Limited for the AI Visual Reference Series.

No part of this publication may be reproduced, stored in a retrieval system, or transmitted in any form or by any means: electronic, mechanical, photocopying, recording, or otherwise, without the prior written permission of the author, except for brief quotations used in scholarly reviews or analysis.

This publication is designed to provide accurate information on the subject matter covered.

It is sold with the understanding that the author is not engaged in rendering legal or other professional services.

Any company and product names used in illustrative examples are purely fictional.

About This Series

Published by AI Awareness Limited, creators of the AI Awareness training programme (aiawareness.ai). This series distills the frameworks used in our enterprise training into a fast, visual, look-it-up format. It's written under a shared series name so that each volume can draw on whichever of our specialists knows that domain best — the same approach used by long-running reference series where consistency of format matters more than a single author's voice.

This is the first title in a growing series, each volume applying the same visual, look-it-up approach to a different professional domain. Titles currently in development include:

- AI in Change Management Visual Reference
- AI in Risk and Audit Visual Reference
- AI in Cybersecurity Visual Reference
- AI in Human Resources Visual Reference
- AI in Financial Institutions Visual Reference
- AI in Healthcare Visual Reference

New titles are added regularly. Search "AI Awareness Visual Reference" or visit **www.aiawareness.ai** for the complete, up-to-date list.

Contents

How to Use This Book

This is not a book meant to be read start to finish in one sitting, and it will not ask you to.

Most business books are written as a single argument: one idea building on the last, chapter by chapter, until you reach a conclusion at the end. This book works differently. Every page stands on its own. Each one takes a single concept, a single question, or a single practical scenario, and gives you what you need to understand it, without requiring you to have read what came before.

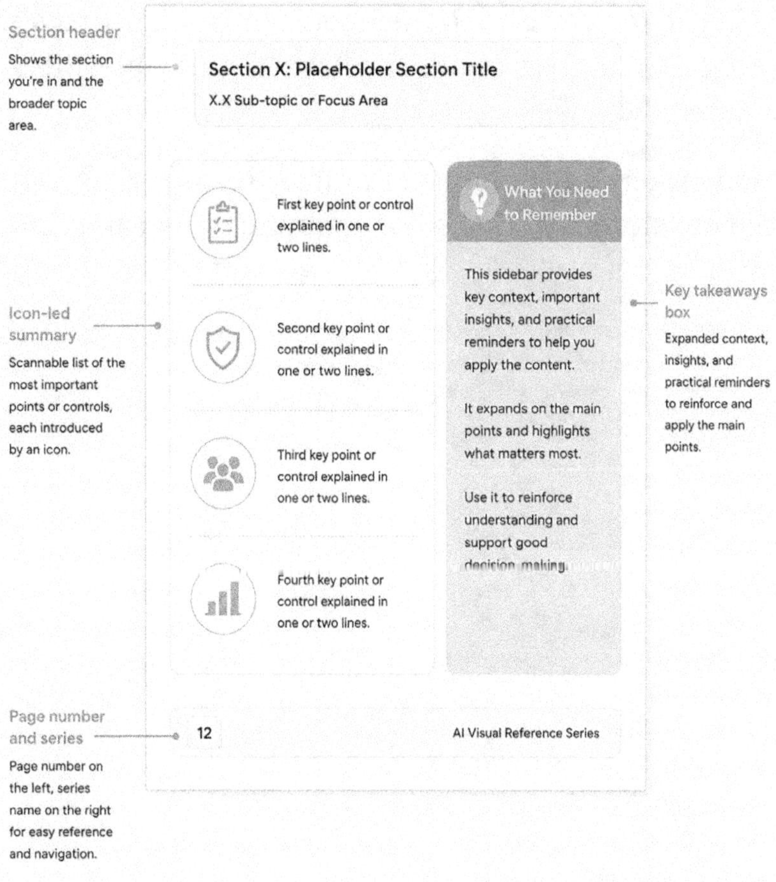

That means you should feel free to jump around. If a section title or a page heading catches your eye, open straight to it. If you are preparing for a specific meeting, facing a specific decision, or simply want a fast answer to a specific question, look it up directly rather than searching for it inside a longer chapter.

The table of contents is built to support this: it is organised by topic, not by a storyline you need to follow in order.

A few conventions repeat throughout the book, so a quick note on what to expect:

- Each section opens with a short page describing what it covers, so you can decide quickly whether it is the one you need.
- Most pages pair a visual, such as a diagram, a checklist, or an icon-led summary, with the practical explanation next to it.
- The visual is there to make the idea easier to scan and easier to recall later, not as decoration.
- Look for the "What You Need to Remember" box on many pages. It distils that page down to the two or three points most worth carrying with you, if that is all the time you have.

Keep this book somewhere you will reach for it again: on a desk, not a shelf. It is designed to be opened dozens of times, for a minute or two at a time, rather than once, cover to cover.

Introduction

Welcome to the AI Awareness: Visual Reference series.

Each book in this series takes a single professional domain and distills it into a format built for how people actually use reference material: not read once and shelved, but opened, scanned, and returned to. Every page pairs a clear visual with the essential point it supports, so a concept that might take three paragraphs to explain in a traditional guide can be grasped in seconds, and located again just as quickly the next time you need it.

This first volume tackles AI governance and ethics: the frameworks, principles, and operational habits that let an organisation use AI safely, responsibly, and in line with its own values. It is a fitting place to start the series, because governance is not really a separate topic from the AI adoption happening across every sector this series will go on to cover. It is the foundation underneath all of it.

The pace of change here has been genuinely fast. Governance built for a single, predictable model does not hold up well against the tools most organisations now use day to day: chatbots, copilots, agents, and workflows that call on multiple systems and take action rather than simply producing an answer.

This book works through what changed, why older frameworks fall short, and what a practical, workable governance approach looks like in 2026: covering the full lifecycle from build to retirement, the roles and accountability that need to be clear before something goes wrong, and the questions worth asking before any new AI use case gets approved.

Nothing here requires a technical background. The visual format is deliberate: AI governance affects far more people in an organisation than the technical team alone, and the ideas that matter most are the ones that hold up when explained plainly and shown clearly, not buried in jargon.

Wherever you are in your own organisation's AI journey, we hope this book earns a place on your desk, not your shelf.

SECTION 1

Modern AI Governance Fundamentals

In this section, we look at what AI governance actually means in 2026 and why the frameworks of the past no longer fit the tools organisations now use every day. Governance is defined as the combination of policies, controls, accountability structures and ongoing oversight that keeps AI use safe, responsible and lawful: an active operational discipline, not a one-time sign-off, spanning how systems are built, deployed, monitored and eventually retired.

A central shift is from governing a single model to governing an entire AI system (a model bundled with prompts, connected tools, data retrieval and a user interface), because large language models, multimodal systems, tool use and agentic behaviour raise questions that legacy, predictive-ML frameworks cannot handle. Five practical objectives anchor the discipline: safety, compliance, trust, value (enabling responsible use rather than merely restricting it) and resilience.

We then survey the current product landscape. ChatGPT spans consumer, Teams and Enterprise tiers, with GPTs, voice and agentic browsing, and staff often adopt personal accounts before any policy exists. Claude offers long-context document processing, Artifacts and MCP connectivity, though deep document handling can expose sensitive content. Microsoft 365 Copilot is embedded across Word, Excel, Teams and Outlook, inheriting the user's permissions and making access control itself a risk. Agent mode across all three shifts AI from answering to acting.

Four principles for responsible use follow: transparency and disclosure, accountability and ownership, fairness and non-discrimination, and human agency and contestability. Finally, we trace governance across the full lifecycle, from intake and use-case approval, through design, prototyping, deployment and operations, to retirement and sunset planning, framed as one connected loop where gaps cluster at the handoffs and mature governance applies proportionate oversight.

Section 1: Modern AI Governance Fundamentals

1.1 What AI Governance Means Now

Defining AI Governance in 2026

- Policies & controls that keep AI safe, responsible, and compliant.
- Covers build, deployment, monitoring, and retirement in real operations.
- Includes employee use of generative tools (e.g., chatbots and office copilots), not only internal ML models.
- Clear accountability: who approved it, who owns it, and what happens if it fails.
- Ongoing oversight, not a one-time approval.

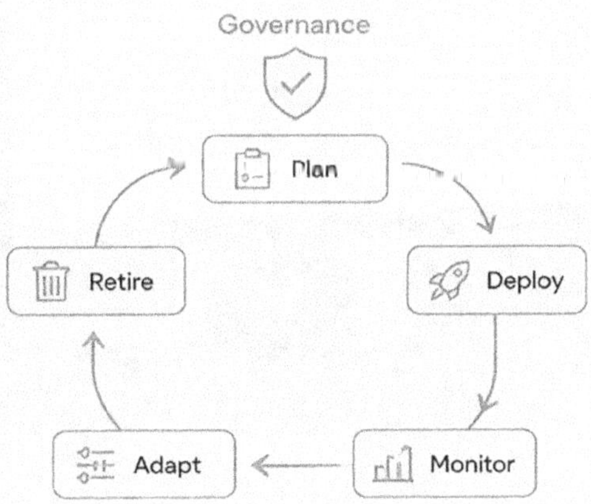

What you Need to Remember

AI governance is a practical, operational discipline—not just a policy document. It helps your organization use AI safely, effectively, and in line with its values and obligations.

It spans the full lifecycle: policies and controls, clear accountability, and ongoing oversight across build, deploy, monitor, adapt, and retire.

Governance applies to the generative AI tools your teams already use every day—document assistants, chat interfaces, analytics copilots—not only your internal ML models.

Accountability and response plans are essential when things go wrong. Everyone should know their role.

Good governance is continuous. It evolves with your tools, your risks, and your organization.

Key Questions

- Is this use safe?
- Who owns the outcome?
- How will we monitor it?

Where Governance Applies

- Document assistants
- Chat interfaces
- Analytics copilots

Your Next Step

Map your current AI tools and owners before new projects launch.

Section 1: Modern AI Governance Fundamentals

1.1 What AI Governance Means Now

From Models to Systems

- Traditional governance focused on a single model's data, accuracy, and bias.
- Today, we govern the entire AI system: model + prompt + tools + data + UI.
- Different experiences—chatbots, copilots, agents, workflows, and APIs—introduce different obligations.
- One product can chain multiple models, retrieval steps, and tool calls, increasing oversight complexity.
- Effective governance means mapping and monitoring every component, not just the core model.

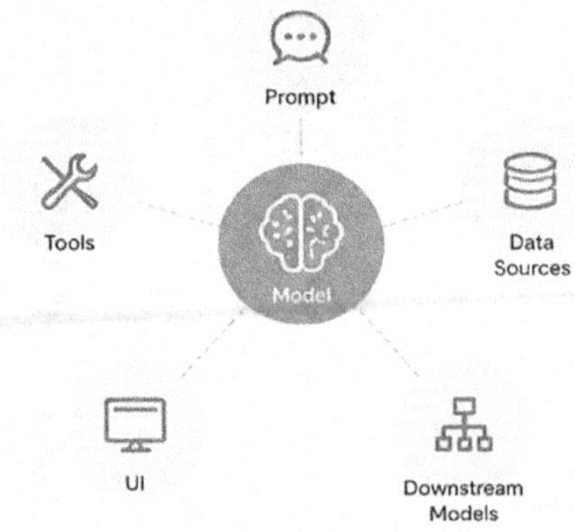

What you Need to Remember

We're moving from model-level checks to system-level governance.

The focus is the whole AI stack deployed in your product—model, prompt, tools, data, UI, and the workflows that connect them.

When systems chain models, retrieval steps, and tool calls, obligations multiply.

Map every component, understand how they interact, and monitor them in production—that's how you govern AI responsibly at scale.

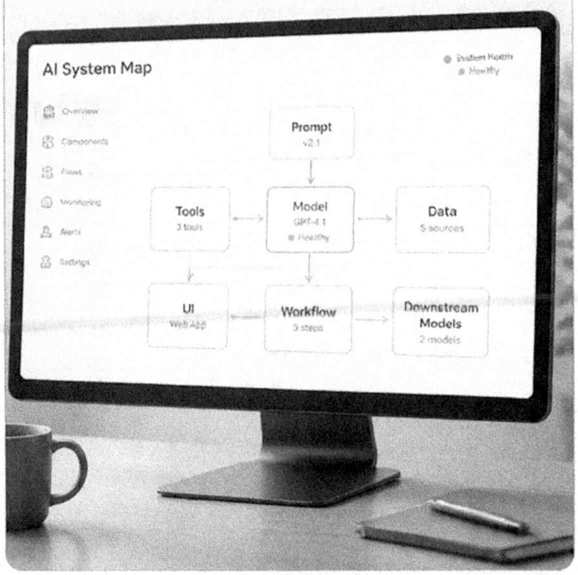

- List all components in your AI system
- Identify where decisions are made
- Check which tools or data sources add risk
- Decide who owns governance for each part

Section 1: Modern AI Governance Fundamentals

1.1 What AI Governance Means Now

Why Old Frameworks Are No Longer Enough

Legacy frameworks focused on structured, predictive ML.

LLMs create open-ended outputs that can't be fully pre-tested.

Multimodal AI expands risk across text, images, audio, documents.

Tool-using models can browse, run code, and call APIs.

Agentic systems pursue multi-step goals, letting risk accumulate.

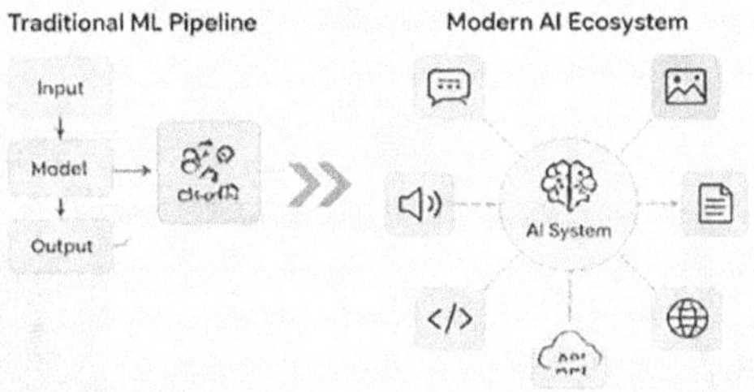

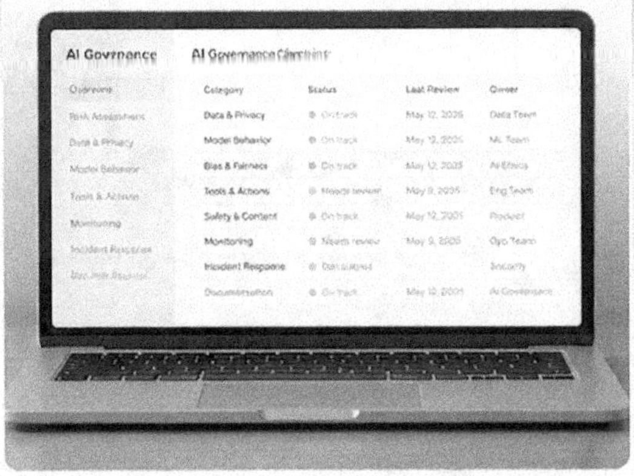

What you Need to Remember

Traditional ML governance assumed fixed inputs and outputs and relied on pre-deployment testing and snapshot reviews.

Today, LLMs, multimodal models, tool use, web access, and agentic behaviors operate across steps and take actions in the real world.

Risk emerges and compounds in dynamic, hard-to-predict ways that old frameworks—and periodic reviews—were never designed to detect.

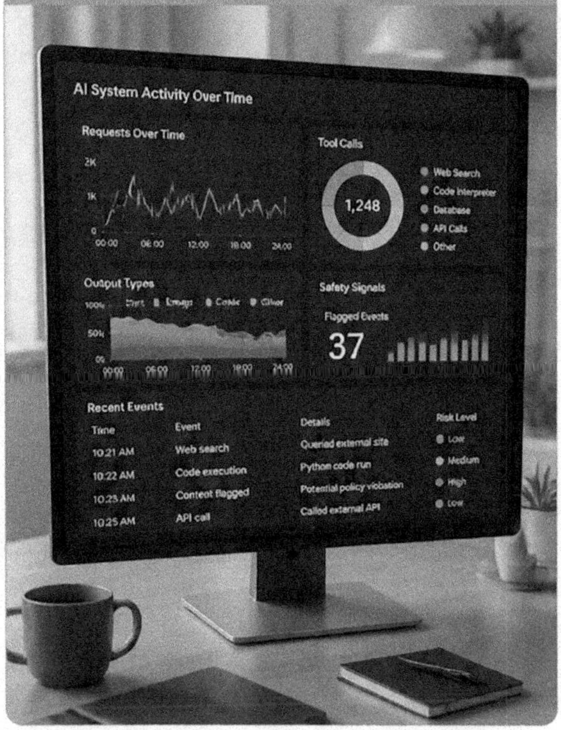

Update governance for: Generative outputs | Tool use & actions | Multimodal data | Agentic workflows

Section 1: Modern AI Governance Fundamentals

1.1 What AI Governance Means Now

Governance Objectives That Matter in Practice

Safety
prevent harm to people, systems, and the organization from AI outputs or actions.

Compliance
meet legal, regulatory, and contractual duties on AI use.

Trust
give stakeholders confidence that AI-assisted processes are reliable and fair.

Value
use governance to enable responsible, high-impact AI, not just limit risk.

Resilience
detect issues early, respond fast, and recover without lasting damage.

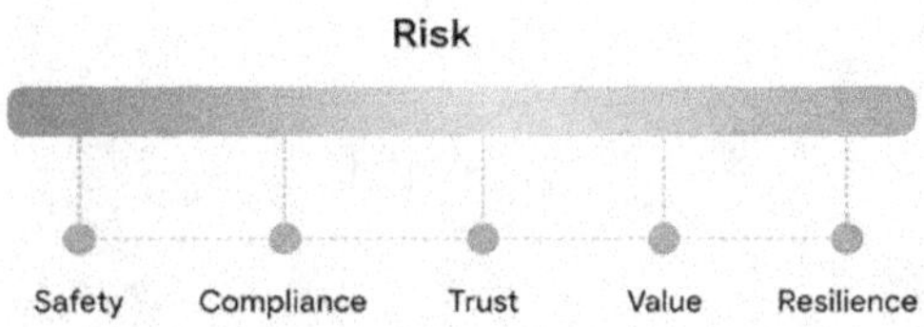

What you Need to Remember

Good AI governance becomes concrete through five measurable objectives that guide everyday decisions.

Safety is the foundation—reducing harm from AI outputs and actions. Compliance ensures we meet legal, regulatory, and contractual requirements on AI use.

Trust combines strong internal controls with transparent, fair outcomes that build confidence with both employees and external stakeholders. Value means using governance to enable responsible, high-impact AI—not to block it.

Resilience is the ability to spot issues early, respond quickly, and recover without lasting damage, so we can keep delivering value even when things go wrong.

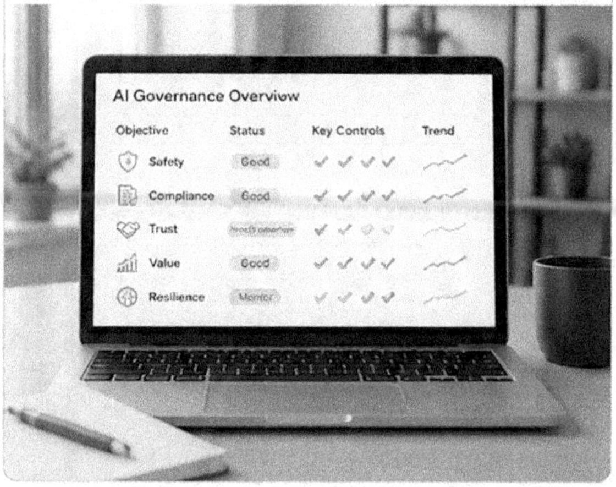

TURNING OBJECTIVES INTO PRACTICE

Define metrics → Set thresholds → Assign owners → Monitor → Review & improve

ChatGPT in Business Contexts

Deployment options
Consumer, Teams, and Enterprise tiers with increasing admin control.

Ways to interact
Chat, voice, canvas editing, and direct file or image uploads.

GPTs & assistants
Pre-configured helpers with custom instructions and tools.

Operator controls
Set guardrails, personas, and connect internal data sources.

Agentic workflows
Let ChatGPT browse, run code, manage files, and call tools.

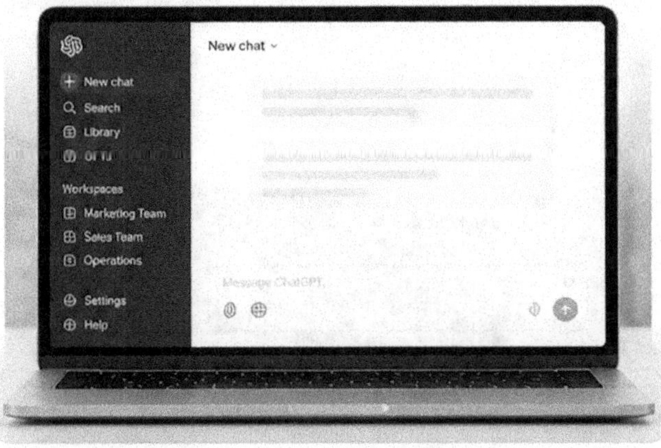

What you Need to Remember

In organisations, ChatGPT functions as a platform, not just a single chatbot window.

Different deployment tiers change how data is handled and who can configure policies, tools, and GPTs.

Most staff arrive with personal accounts already in use, so governance needs to catch up with reality.

Personal use → Team use → Enterprise platform

Useful follow-ups

- Map where ChatGPT is already used today
- Define allowed tools, data sources, and topics
- Plan onboarding for Teams or Enterprise accounts

Section 1: Modern AI Governance Fundamentals

1.2 The Current AI Product Landscape

Claude in Knowledge and Office Workflows

Built by Anthropic
Available via claude.ai, API, and enterprise deployments

Long-context analysis
Ingest full contracts, policies, and reports in one go

Artifacts
Generate editable docs, sheets, slides, and code next to the chat

Extended thinking
Let Claude reason through complex, multi-step problems

MCP connections
Securely connect Claude to internal tools and data

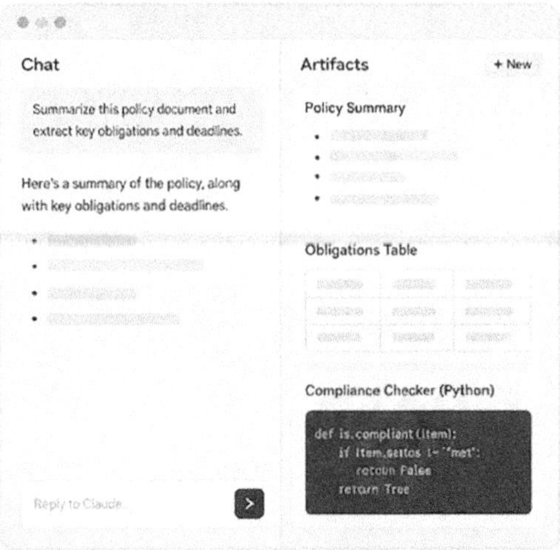

What you Need to Remember

Claude excels at work that requires reading, comparing, and reasoning over large amounts of text — from contracts and policies to reports and research.

Use Artifacts to turn insights into structured outputs like documents, spreadsheets, slides, or code that you can edit and reuse.

Extended thinking helps Claude break down complex, multi-step problems and show its reasoning before giving a final answer.

MCP connections let Claude securely access your internal tools and data, turning it into powered hub for enterprise workflows.

With great capability comes greater risk — connecting to systems and handling sensitive documents increases the need for strong governance, access controls, and audit trails.

Use Claude for: reviewing long documents

Drafting structured outputs

Safe use: never paste sensitive data without approval

Microsoft 365 Copilot in Daily Work

- Copilot is built into Word, Excel, PowerPoint, Outlook, Teams, OneNote.
- Word: drafts, rewrites, summarizes with your org's content.
- Excel: turns plain language into formulas, summaries, charts.
- Teams: summarizes meetings, actions, Q&A from transcript.
- Uses Microsoft Graph to pull emails, files, calendars, chats you can already access.
- Governance risk: if access is too open, Copilot can surface sensitive content.

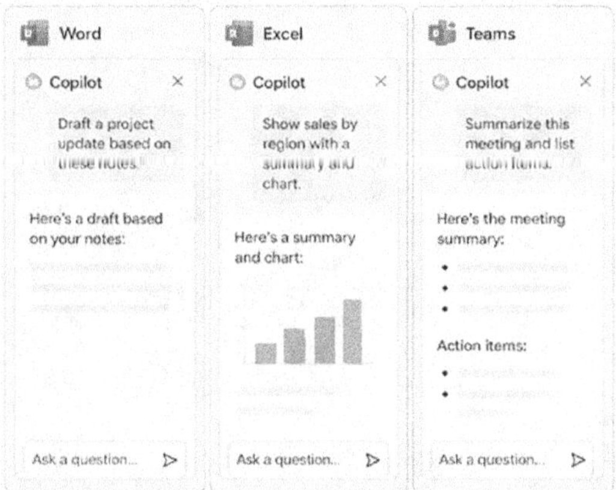

What you Need to Remember

Copilot works inside everyday Microsoft 365 apps, helping write documents, analyze spreadsheets, and capture meetings without learning a new tool.

You still own the quality: always review drafts, formulas, charts, and meeting summaries before sharing or acting on them.

Copilot can only see what you can see, via Microsoft Graph permissions—but broad internal sharing means it may surface documents or chats that are technically accessible but not appropriate to reuse. Good data access governance is essential.

Use Copilot for: drafting, summarizing, exploring data, meeting notes

Double-check: facts, numbers, tone

Governance actions: tighten sharing, review permissions, train teams

Agent Mode Across Workplace Tools

Goal-driven across steps and tools
Agent mode pursues your objective across multiple steps and applications until it's complete or blocked.

ChatGPT agents chain capabilities
Browse the web, run code, analyse data, and manage files—chaining tools to get the job done.

Claude agents use your computer
Operate the desktop and connect to systems through MCP to complete real-world tasks.

Copilot agents automate work
In Microsoft 365, agents handle recurring work like reports, inbox triage, and retrieval across business data.

Different levels of human oversight
Agents can run with full supervision, approval at key points, or minimal oversight as policies allow.

Higher stakes when AI takes action
When agents act in your systems, mistakes can have real consequences.

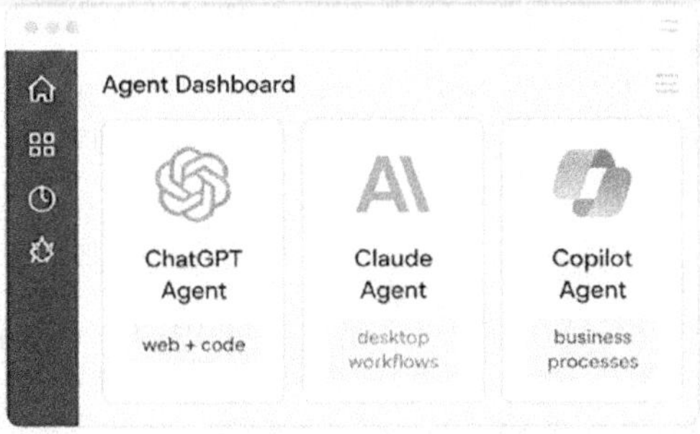

Assistant mode waits for your prompt and returns an answer—usually text.

Agent mode is different. You give it a goal. The agent plans the work, uses the right tools, takes actions in your systems, and continues until the goal is complete or it's blocked.

ChatGPT agents can browse the web, run code, analyse data, create files, and chain tools together to complete complex tasks.

Claude agents can operate your desktop and use MCP-connected systems to perform actions across applications and databases.

Microsoft 365 Copilot agents can automate business processes—like generating reports, triaging inboxes, and retrieving information—from across the Microsoft 365 ecosystem.

What you Need to Remember

- Agents act, not just answer. They can take real actions in your tools and systems.
- They can run with little or no human oversight, depending on how they're configured.
- Mis-configured agents can send emails, edit files, update records, or submit forms.
- Clear guardrails, approvals, and permissions reduce risk.
- Monitor activity, review results, and iterate policies as agents evolve.

Ongoing inbox triage	Scheduled reports	Data retrieval from multiple systems	Updating trackers or logs	Monitoring for defined events

1.3 Core Principles for Responsible AI Use

Flag when AI is in the loop
People have a right to know when AI shaped content or a decision that affects them.

Match disclosure to context
Customer chatbots, employee tools, and analytics dashboards need different levels of clarity.

Go beyond labels
Say what the AI actually did and where its output may be incomplete or wrong.

Protect trust and compliance
Hiding AI involvement can erode trust and increase legal or regulatory risk.

Use the practical rule
If knowing AI was involved would change what someone does, tell them clearly.

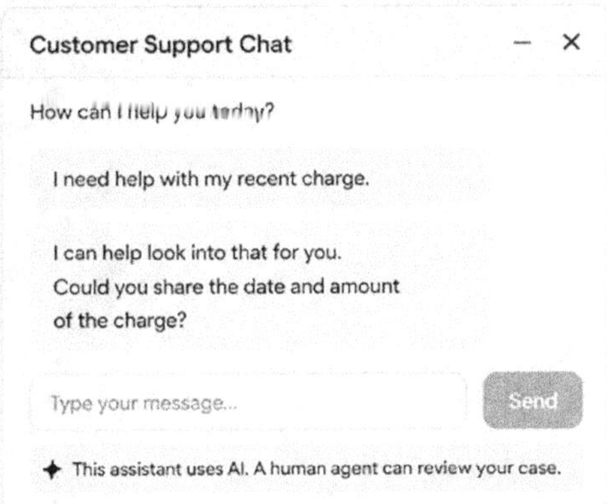

What you Need to Remember

Start from impact: anyone affected by an AI-assisted decision deserves to know it was in the loop.

Disclosure looks different for public chatbots, internal drafting tools, and analytics — but it's always required when it might change what people decide or how they respond.

Transparency means explaining what the AI did, where it can be unreliable, and who is accountable.

Skipping disclosure risks loss of trust and, in regulated areas, legal consequences.

QUICK CHECKS BEFORE YOU USE AI OUTPUT

- Would this look different if people knew AI was involved?
- Is there any legal, policy, or customer expectation to disclose?
- Have we made it easy to ask for a human review?

Accountability and Ownership

- Responsibility sits with people and organisations, not the AI system.
- Assign who is accountable before deployment, not after an incident.
- Ownership includes: the AI output, the decisions based on it, and any resulting harms.
- Agentic workflows increase hand-offs, so map the chain of accountability clearly.
- Governance must state who is accountable at each stage of the AI lifecycle.

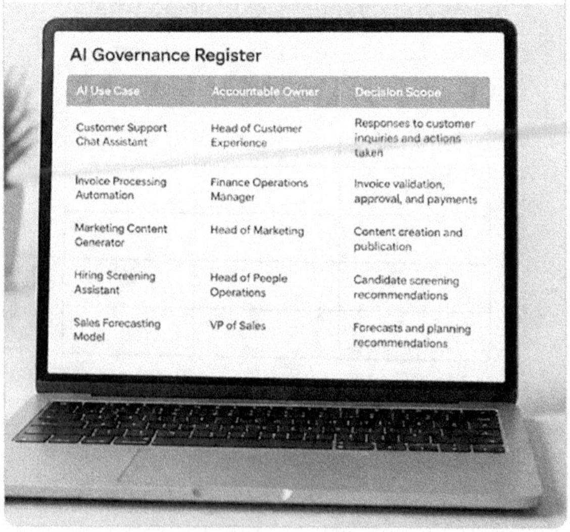

What you Need to Remember

AI does not dilute responsibility—people and organisations remain accountable for how systems are designed, used, and acted upon.

Accountability must be set in advance. Decide who owns the outputs, who can approve actions, and who bears responsibility if things go wrong.

Ownership extends beyond the model. It covers the AI outputs, the decisions those outputs inform, and any resulting benefits or harms.

Agentic and multi-step workflows introduce more hand-offs and dependencies. Build explicit governance that maps the chain of accountability and names the owner at each stage.

- Name an accountable owner for every AI deployment
- Keep an accessible record of who owns which decisions
- Review accountability when workflows or tools change

Fairness and Non-Discrimination

- AI can inherit bias from training data, prompts, and retrieval sources.
- Skewed patterns usually appear only at scale, not in single answers.
- Highest risk areas: hiring, lending, performance scoring, customer eligibility.
- Fairness needs structured testing, not just 'no bad intent.'
- Define what 'fair' means for your organisation before deploying AI in sensitive workflows.

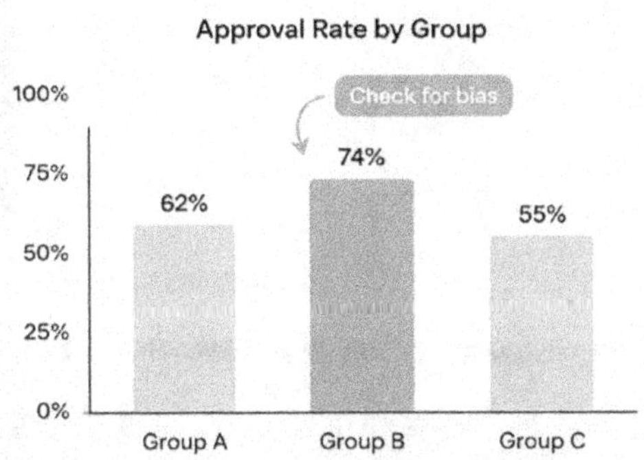

Look for patterns across groups, not individual cases.

What you Need to Remember

AI learns from historical data, so it can quietly reproduce past inequalities. The real risk is in decisions that shape people's opportunities: hiring tools, credit checks, performance scores, customer triage.

Individual outputs may look fine, while the overall pattern disadvantages a group. Fairness means testing outcomes at the population level, agreeing clear fairness metrics up front, and only then deploying models into sensitive workflows.

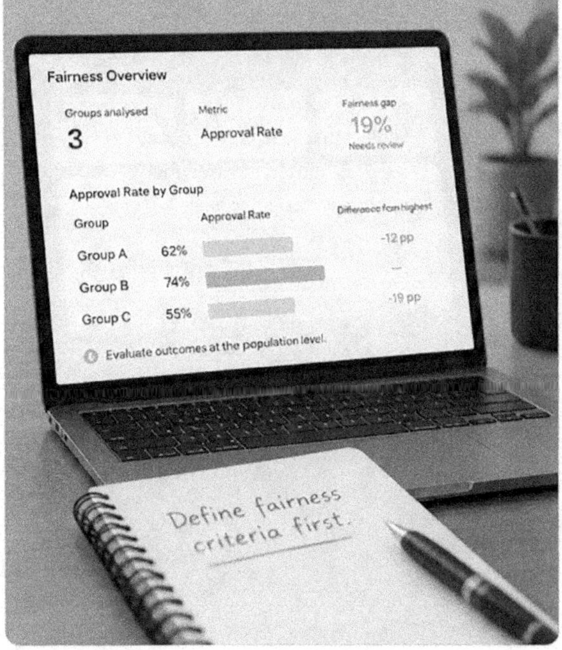

- When to check for bias: before launch, after major model changes, and on a regular schedule.
- Bring in diverse reviewers and domain experts for fairness testing.
- Escalate issues quickly—update data, prompts, or workflows to correct unfair patterns.

Human Agency and Contestability

People affected by AI-assisted decisions need information to understand, question and override them.

Human agency = real control: time, authority and options, not box-ticking oversight.

Contestability needs simple, visible routes for review and appeal.

Treat automation bias as a governance risk, not 'user error'.

High-stakes uses must build in explicit human review and override steps.

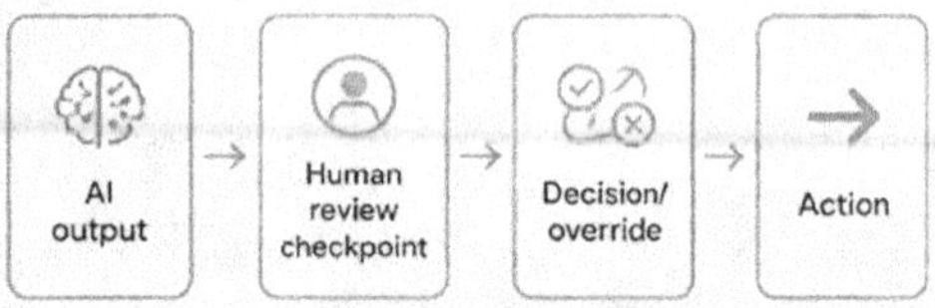

What you Need to Remember

Keep humans genuinely in control. Seeing an AI recommendation isn't enough — people need context, time and authority to question it. Build clear ways for staff and affected individuals to challenge outcomes and trigger review.

Watch for automation bias: when AI feels 'always right', scrutiny disappears.

For any decision about jobs, health, money or legal status, require a named human decision-maker and a documented override option before action is taken.

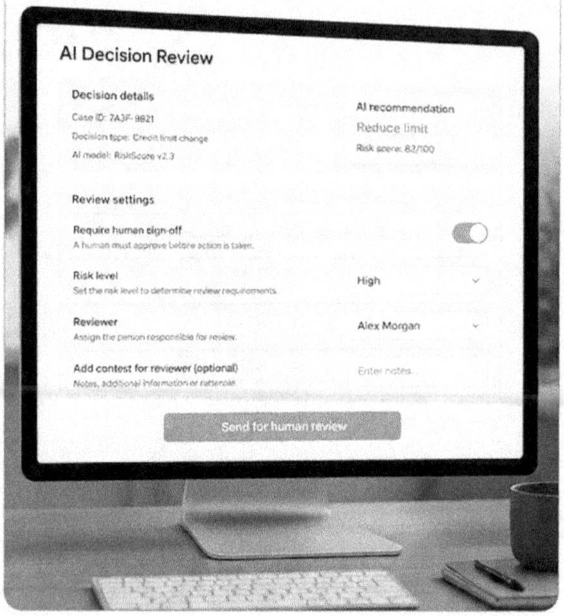

Ask: Who can override this AI — and how easy is it?

Map review checkpoints into high-stakes workflows.

Train teams to spot and challenge automation bias.

1.4 Governance Across the AI Lifecycle

Intake and Use-Case Approval

Start with formal intake, not a sprint
Capture key details upfront to avoid rework and missed risks.

Capture purpose, data, people, and potential harms
Make the context and impact clear from the beginning.

Use intake as the first governance gate
Ensure only well-scoped, necessary ideas move forward.

Require stronger justification for high-risk use cases
Apply proportional scrutiny based on risk level.

Create an audit-ready record from day one
Build a clear paper trail for transparency and accountability.

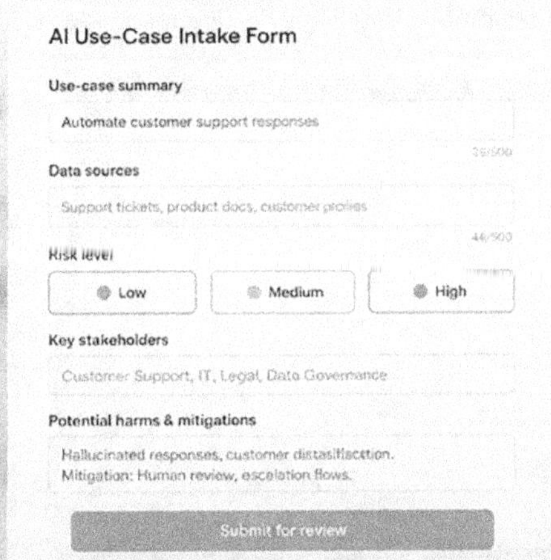

What you Need to Remember

Intake is your first checkpoint. It brings structure and discipline to the earliest stage of an AI idea before any build begins.

It helps filter out unclear, unnecessary, or duplicative ideas and ensures the right context is captured upfront.

Apply proportional scrutiny based on risk—higher-risk use cases require deeper justification, stronger safeguards, and broader stakeholder review.

A complete intake creates a paper trail that supports decisions, enables audits, and builds trust across your organization.

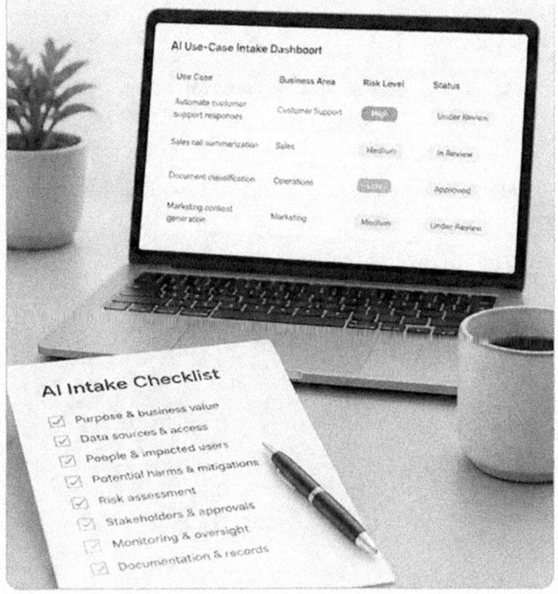

When to use intake: New AI idea | Change to data or users | Escalated risk | Regulatory request

Deciding What Should and Should Not Be Built

Approval is a real decision — someone owns the yes/no.

Reject when data use is prohibited, risk is too high, or oversight is unclear.

Use conditional "yes, if..." approvals that add specific controls.

Include legal, security, compliance and business voices — not just IT.

Log every approved use case in a central register for visibility.

AI Use Case Register

Use case	Owner	Risk level	Status	Next review
Invoice processing assistant	Finance Ops	Low	Approved	15 Jun 2025
Customer feedback analysis	CX Insights	Medium	Conditional	22 Jul 2025
HR policy summariser	People Ops	Medium	Conditional	10 Jul 2025
Candidate screening co-pilot	Talent Acquisition	High	Rejected	—
Contract clause extraction	Legal	High	Rejected	—

What you Need to Remember

Every AI use case needs a clear, accountable decision-maker. Automatic approval is just theatre and creates risk without adding any control.

Say no when the data is impermissible to use, the risk is too high compared to the controls, or there is no credible human review. Any one of these is a valid reason to pause.

Conditional approvals with specific controls turn "maybe" into a managed path forward. Cross-functional panels surface blind spots, balance perspectives, and build trust.
Keep a live register of all approved use cases so you always know what's running, under what conditions, and when it's due for review.

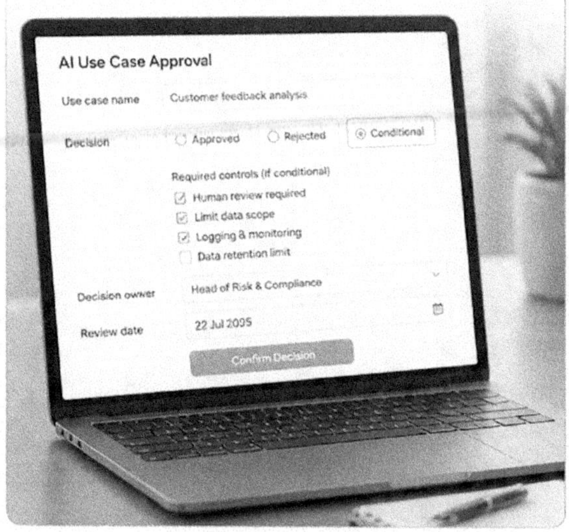

Ask: Should we build this at all?

Decide: Who owns the risk and the yes/no?

Track: Add every approved use case to the register.

1.4 Governance Across the AI Lifecycle

Design and Prototyping Controls

- Build governance into design, not just deployment.
- Define safe prompting rules before any tests.
- Set strict data boundaries for prototypes.
- Use approval checkpoints before real users or data.
- Document intended behaviour, constraints, and rationale.

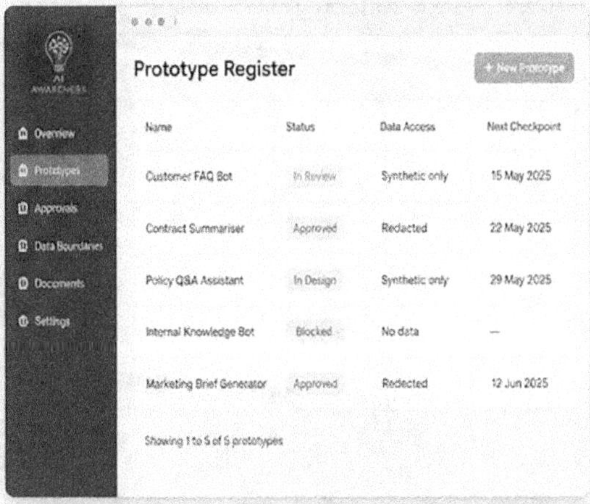

What you Need to Remember

Good governance starts in the design phase. Treat prototypes as governed assets, not experiments outside the rules.

Define safe prompting rules before any testing begins. This includes what users can ask, what the model can do, and how it should respond.

Set strict data boundaries for every prototype. Use synthetic or redacted data by default and limit access to only what's necessary.

Require approval checkpoints before exposing a prototype to real users or any real data. No shortcuts.

Document the intended behaviour, constraints, and rationale. Clear documentation is your baseline for reviews, approvals, and audits.

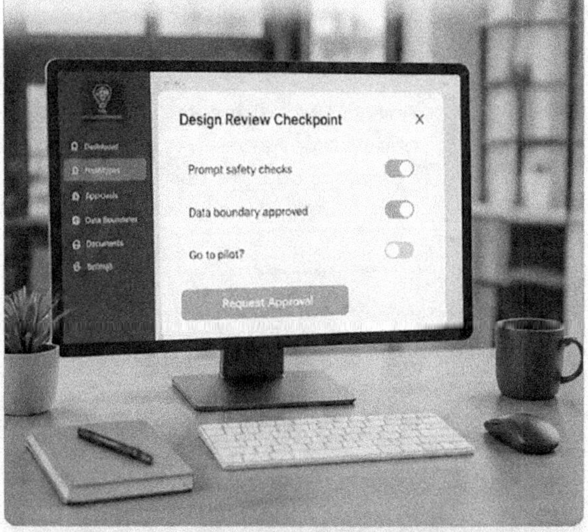

Controls at every stage

Design → Prototype → Pilot → Production

Minimum controls for prototypes

- Safe prompts
- Limited data
- Named owner

Never connect prototypes directly to live customer data.

Boundaries, and Approval Checkpoints

- System prompts set AI operating boundaries — treat them as governance artefacts.
- Version-control, review, and approve prompts before team-wide or scaled use.
- Define data boundaries: what can go in, what may appear in outputs, who can see what.
- Tie approval checkpoints to key milestones: proof of concept, internal pilot, pre-production.
- Any change to prompts or data scope after approval triggers re-review.

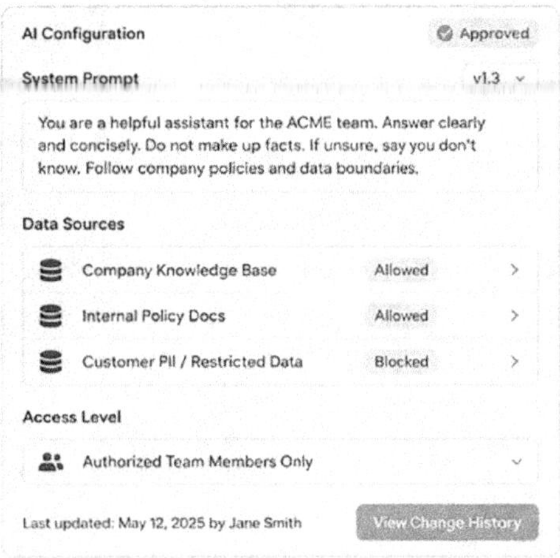

What you Need to Remember

System prompts are high-impact governance documents that set how AI behaves. Treat them with the same rigour as any policy.

Data boundaries must clearly specify what information can be used as input, what may appear in outputs, and who is allowed to see those outputs.

Approval checkpoints should align with key lifecycle milestones — proof of concept, internal pilot, and pre-production — to control risk as you scale.

Even small changes to prompts or data scope can significantly change outcomes and risk. Any change after approval must trigger a re-review before continued use.

- Lock prompts before scale.
- Enforce data boundaries in tools, not just policy.
- Don't skip checkpoints when things change.

Deployment and Operations

Operations start at go-live
Handover to operations with a clear runbook, KPIs, and success criteria.

Monitor output, usage, and odd behaviour
Track model quality, user activity, and anomalies continuously.

Predefined escalation paths
Know who decides, who acts, and the communication plan.

Clear rollback options
Maintain tested rollback plans and fast, safe deployment reversions.

Named production owner
One accountable owner for health, decisions, and outcomes.

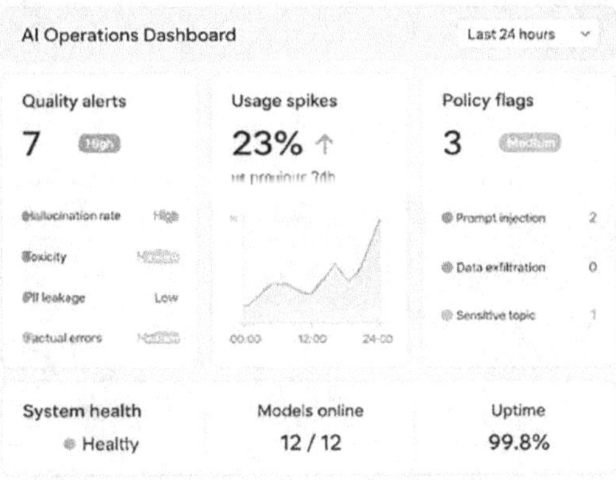

What you Need to Remember

AI governance doesn't end at launch — it continues every day in production.

Monitor model quality, user behaviour, and system signals to catch issues early and spot unexpected outcomes.

Escalation paths must be pre-agreed so the right people can act quickly.

Rollback options must be tested and ready to protect users and the business.

One named owner is accountable for the health of the AI system and for decisions in production.

Before go-live: define monitoring, escalation, rollback, owner.

During operations: review alerts and usage patterns regularly.

After incidents: capture lessons and update controls.

Monitoring, Escalation, and Rollback Procedures

Automated monitoring
Continuously track model behaviour and system performance.

Key signals to watch
Quality, safety, drift, latency, usage, and user feedback.

Escalation thresholds
Define clear thresholds that trigger incident escalation.

Rehearsed rollback plans
Have tested procedures to safely revert or degrade.

Post-incident learning
Review incidents, capture learnings, and strengthen controls.

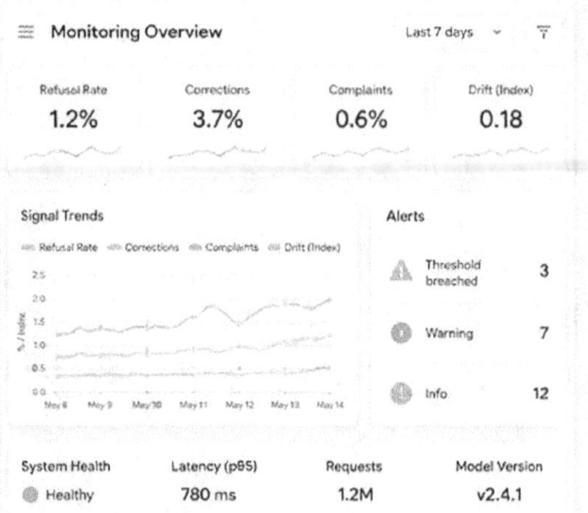

What you Need to Remember

Automated monitoring catches issues at scale, but targeted human review provides the context and judgement AI can't.

Focus on the signals that predict real harm. Clear escalation thresholds turn noisy data into timely, actionable incidents.

Rollback plans must be tested so recovery is fast and safe. Post-incident reviews capture root causes and drive continuous improvement.

1 Monitor — Track key signals daily.

2 Escalate — Trigger action at defined thresholds.

3 Roll Back & Learn — Rehearse rollback, update designs.

Retirement and Replacement

Plan for the end, not just the launch.

Know your retirement triggers: deprecation, regulation, performance, risk.

Start sunset planning early—before urgency hits.

Treat replacements as new systems with full intake and approval.

Govern data, logs, and outputs when systems are decommissioned.

AI System Retirement Dashboard — All Systems

System	Trigger	Target Retirement Date	Owner	Status
Demand Forecast Model v1	Vendor deprecation	2025-06-30	Data Ops	On Track
Customer Support Assistant (v2)	Performance drift	2025-08-15	CX Ops	At Risk
Pricing Optimizer	Regulation change	2025-09-30	Risk & Compliance	On Track
Content Generator	Risk profile shift	2025-11-30	Legal	Delayed
Fraud Detection Model v1	Vendor deprecation	2025-12-31	Security	On Track

View Retirement Plan >

What you Need to Remember

Retirement is a distinct and high-risk phase in the AI lifecycle. Many organisations focus on building and scaling solutions, but neglect planning for how and when to retire them.

Common retirement triggers include a vendor deprecating a model, regulatory changes, performance degradation or drift, and shifts in the system's risk profile.

Sunset timelines must be deliberate. Evaluate replacement systems as new solutions with full intake and approval. When decommissioning, ensure prompts, logs, training data, and outputs are governed and disposed of in line with policy and legal requirements.

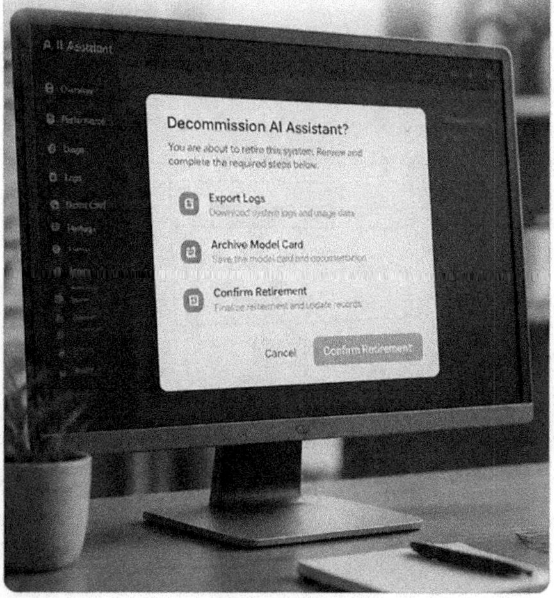

Before launch: define retirement triggers and data disposal rules.

During use: regularly review performance, risk, and regulatory fit.

At end-of-life: execute sunset plan, confirm data clean-up, document lessons learned.

Sunset Planning for Outdated or Risky AI Systems

- Define the sunset plan at go-live – not when the system starts failing.
- Name a retirement owner with clear decision authority.
- Specify trigger conditions: risk thresholds, performance drops, or policy changes.
- Set an indicative timeline for notice, transition, and shutdown.
- Map user and workflow dependencies before decommissioning.
- Plan the transition path: replacements, manual workarounds, data migration.
- Schedule a post-retirement audit for data retention/deletion and access closure.
- Capture lessons learned to improve governance of successor systems.

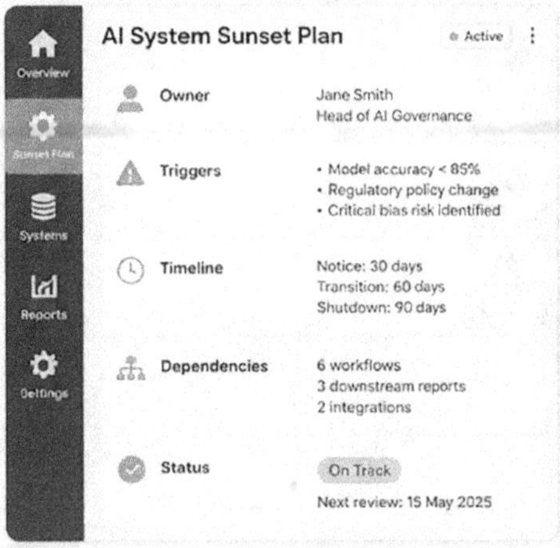

What you Need to Remember

A sunset plan is a structured decommissioning document. It should be produced during deployment, so everyone knows from day one how the AI system will be retired.

Every plan needs four anchors: who owns the retirement decision, what events will trigger it, how long each phase will take, and how users and workflows will transition.

Treat communication as a governance responsibility. Give heavy users more notice, and coordinate updates across business, risk, and IT so no one is surprised when access changes.

Before shutdown, map hidden dependencies – integrations, automations, and reports that quietly rely on the AI system – and design alternatives.

After shutdown, confirm that data and outputs follow policy and that nothing critical still points at the retired system. Feed lessons into the organisation's AI governance playbook.

Use This Checklist When...

- Approving a new AI deployment
- Reviewing an ageing or high-risk AI tool
- Planning migrations to a successor system

Section 1: Modern AI Governance Fundamentals

1.4 Governance Across the AI Lifecycle

The Lifecycle as a Governance System

- **One connected loop, not four separate processes**
- **Each stage's quality depends on the one before**
- **Risks cluster at handoffs between stages**
- **Oversight should match the stakes at each stage**
- **Treat lifecycle governance as an ongoing discipline**

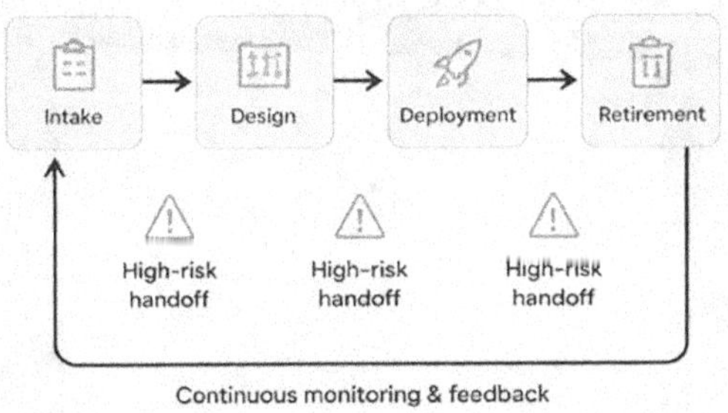

What you Need to Remember

AI governance is a system, not a checklist. Weaknesses at any stage propagate forward, compounding risk and limiting control.

Transitions—design to deployment, pilot to scale, and active to decommissioning—are danger points where assumptions break and risk can spike.

Apply proportional rigour across the lifecycle. Early choices set the foundation, but vigilance is needed throughout to keep systems safe, effective, and aligned with purpose.

Mature organisations monitor and re-review continuously, using feedback and change triggers to adapt governance as systems and contexts evolve.

When to review lifecycle governance

New high-risk use case	Major model update	Incident or near-miss	Change in regulation	Third-party dependency change

Low-Risk vs High-Risk AI Use Cases

1. Risk varies by impact + **reversibility — start classification here.**
2. Low-risk: internal drafts, summarisation, brainstorming, personal productivity.
3. Medium-risk: client-facing content, data analysis, advice that informs decisions.
4. High-risk: automated decisions about people, medical triage, credit, hiring, legal advice.
5. Document the risk level **and revisit as use cases** evolve.

Low	Medium	High
Low impact, reversible, individual use.	Moderate impact, informs decisions, client or team implications.	High impact, affects people's lives, rights or livelihoods.

What you Need to Remember

- Match oversight to potential harm — that's practical AI governance.
- Don't treat every AI use the same: over-restriction kills value; under-restriction creates exposure.
- Low-risk: internal, reversible, low-stakes. Medium-risk: shapes client decisions. High-risk: directly affects people's lives, livelihoods, or rights.
- Risk isn't fixed — review classifications regularly as tools and contexts change.

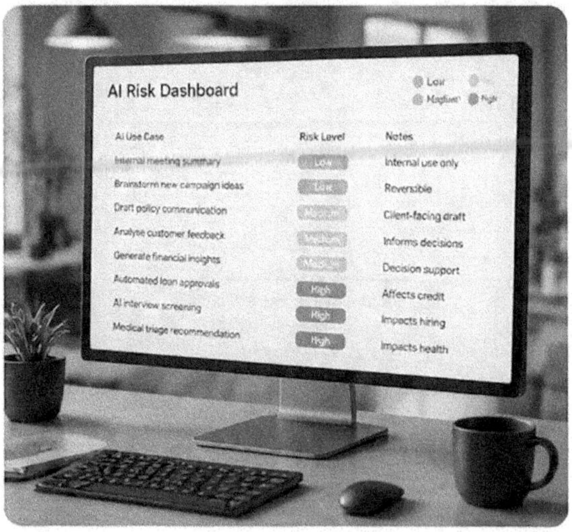

- Define examples of low/medium/high risk for your team.
- Schedule regular reviews of AI use cases.
- Escalate high-risk ideas for expert or legal review before deployment.

Risk Dimensions That Matter

Accuracy risk – AI outputs that are wrong, misleading, or not grounded in sources.

Privacy risk – Personal or sensitive data exposed through prompts or files.

Bias risk – Unequal or discriminatory outcomes across groups.

Security risk – Prompt injection, data leakage, or unauthorized access.

Autonomy risk – AI taking actions without enough human review.

Legal exposure – IP, liability, or regulatory non-compliance.

Risk checklist

- [ ] Accuracy risk
- [ ] Privacy risk
- [ ] Bias risk
- [ ] Security risk
- [ ] Autonomy risk
- [ ] Legal exposure

What you Need to Remember

Match controls to the risks in play.

Each AI use case exposes a different mix of risks. The more clearly you understand the use case, the better you can match safeguards that fit.

Accuracy and privacy risks are the most common when people rely blindly on AI outputs or paste real customer or employee data into tools without thinking.

Bias, security, autonomy, and legal exposure become critical when AI evaluates people, makes recommendations, or takes actions across systems and processes.

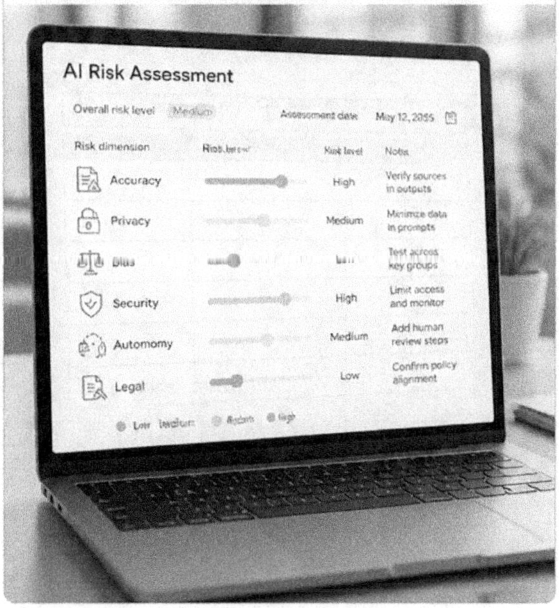

Quick Uses for this Cheat Sheet

- Designing a new AI use case
- Reviewing vendor tools
- Planning controls with risk owners
- Explaining risks to business teams

Section 1: Modern AI Governance Fundamentals

1.5 Risk-Based Thinking for AI

Risk Tolerance and Governance Thresholds

Define acceptable residual risk
Decide what level of impact and likelihood the business can live with.

Make thresholds explicit
Document criteria, not gut feel in the moment.

Below-threshold use
Frictionless: simple guidelines, light review, trust in users.

Above-threshold use
Formal approval, extra controls, or restriction.

Consider cumulative risk
Low-risk tasks can add up across teams and workflows.

Align leadership first
Board and execs agree the tolerance before you set rules.

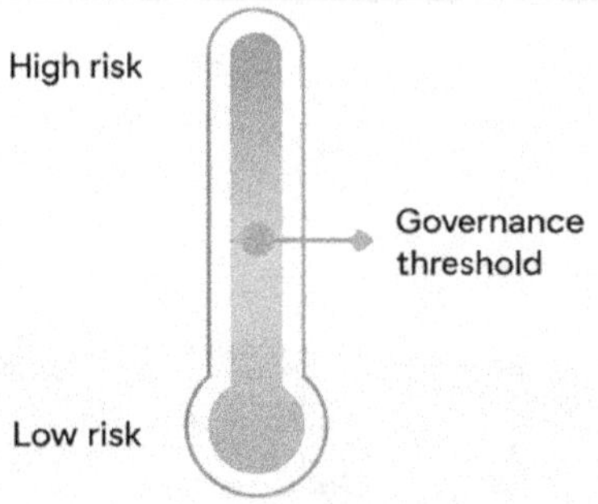

What you Need to Remember

Risk tolerance is what turns AI governance from theory into operational decisions.

Below the threshold, AI use should feel fast and low-friction—simple guidelines, light review, and trust in users.

Above the threshold, governance machinery activates—bringing in legal, security, or technical review, extra controls, or restrictions.

Thresholds must reflect aggregate risk across the organisation, not just individual tasks.

Ultimately, risk tolerance is a business decision. Leadership ownership is essential to set the right bar and stand by it.

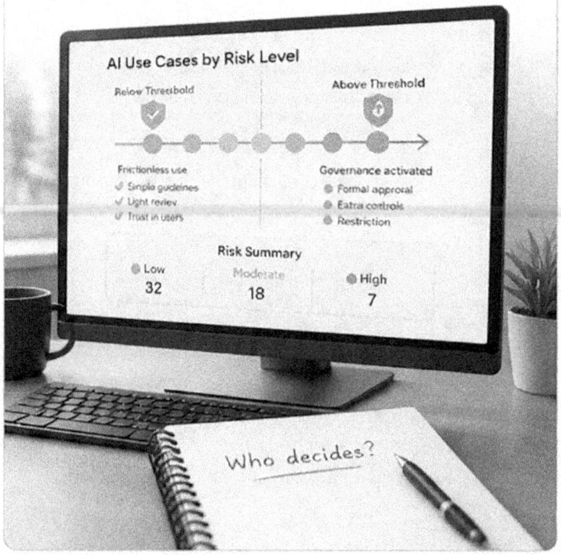

Use impact + likelihood to size risk.

Scan for aggregate and systemic risk.

Define who approves above-threshold AI.

Governance by Scenario

1 Drafting – low autonomy, high human review

Controls: accuracy checks, tone review.

2 Analysis – medium autonomy

Controls: data quality, clear sources, verification.

3 Recommendations – higher stakes

Controls: bias checks, conflict-of-interest, sign-off.

4 Action-taking – highest risk

Controls: tight scope limits, explicit approval, audit trail.

Same tool, different risk

Drafting → Analysis → Recommendations → Actions

RISK INCREASES

What you Need to Remember

Good governance follows the task, not just the tool.

As you move from drafting to analysis, recommendations, and action-taking, the impact and risk increase.

That's why controls should tighten at each step—so decisions stay accurate, fair, and accountable.

Start simple, add the right controls, and always leave a clear record of how and why decisions were made.

- Clarify the task
- Set the right controls
- Document decisions

SECTION 2

Law, Policy, and Standards for AI Governance

In this section, we look at the external rules and internal policies that shape how organisations govern AI. We begin with the major legal frameworks: the EU AI Act and its four-tier risk pyramid (from banned applications down to minimal-risk uses); the largely voluntary US approach anchored by the NIST AI Risk Management Framework (Govern, Map, Measure, Manage); the UK's principles-based route through existing regulators; China's targeted rules; and ISO/IEC 42001, the first certifiable AI management standard.

We then turn to demonstrating compliance through audit trails, decision records, internal assurance versus external audit, and evidence packs tailored to regulators, clients and boards. A substantial part is practical policy-making:

Acceptable Use Policies covering approved and prohibited uses; model and vendor approval gateways, where the data-processing question (whether inputs are used for training) is most critical; employee prompting guidance built on data minimisation and prompt libraries; and policy refresh cycles that keep documents current as tools evolve.

The section closes on responsible procurement, since most organisations buy rather than build AI: due diligence to surface embedded AI features, vendor transparency and certifications, the open-source versus proprietary choice, and shared responsibility across provider, platform, organisation and user.

The EU AI Act in Practice

- World's first comprehensive, binding AI law
- Four risk tiers: unacceptable, high, limited, minimal
- Unacceptable: social scoring, real-time biometric tracking in public
- High-risk uses (hiring, credit, healthcare) need documentation, human oversight, transparency, conformity checks
- General-purpose / foundation models must disclose capabilities and key training data information

What you Need to Remember

The EU AI Act is the world's first comprehensive, binding law on artificial intelligence.

It bans certain AI uses that pose unacceptable risks, and imposes strict requirements on high-risk systems—such as those used in hiring, credit scoring, or healthcare.

For general-purpose AI and foundation models, it introduces transparency rules—requiring providers to disclose capabilities and key information about the training data used.

The Act applies to any organisation—inside or outside the EU—that places AI systems on the EU market or whose outputs affect people in the EU.

Non-compliance can lead to very high fines (up to €35 million or 7% of global annual turnover, whichever is higher).

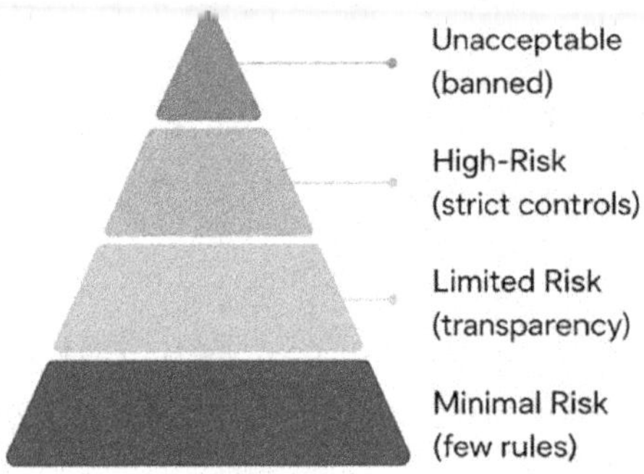

- Check if your AI system is 'high-risk' before launch.
- Keep documentation, data sources and human-oversight processes auditable.
- If your AI touches EU users, assume you're in scope and get legal advice.

Section 2: Law, Policy, and Standards for AI Governance

2.1 The Global Regulatory Landscape

NIST AI RMF and Related US Approaches

US AI GOVERNANCE AT A GLANCE

- Sector-led, mostly voluntary approach — no single binding AI law.
- NIST AI Risk Management Framework (AI RMF) as the core reference.
- Four functions: Govern, Map, Measure, Manage.
- Govern = accountability; Map = context; Measure = assess; Manage = respond.
- Sector regulators (FDA, CFPB, EEOC, SEC) apply existing laws to AI.
- Executive actions and state laws (esp. California) fill the gaps.

HOW IT WORKS IN PRACTICE

The NIST AI Risk Management Framework (AI RMF) is the US government's practical playbook for managing AI risk. It is voluntary, flexible, and designed to be used by any organization, regardless of size or sector.

Organizations use the AI RMF to set governance and accountability, map their AI systems and impacts, measure and assess risks, and manage those risks with mitigations and controls.

Oversight is distributed across domain regulators—such as the FDA (medical devices), CFPB (consumer finance), EEOC (employment), and SEC (securities)—who apply existing laws and rules to AI within their jurisdictions.

There is no comprehensive federal AI law yet. Executive orders and federal guidance direct agencies to act, while states—especially California—are enacting AI-specific requirements that add another layer of obligations.

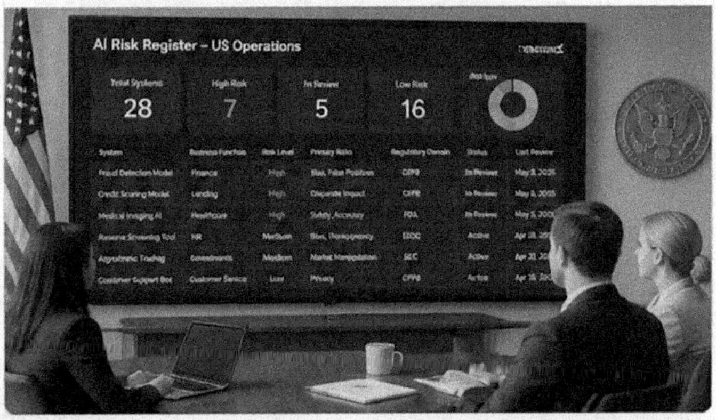

WHAT YOU NEED TO REMEMBER

- AI oversight in the US is distributed and sector-based—multiple agencies apply existing laws to AI in their domains.
- NIST AI RMF is the central, flexible framework organizations use to manage AI risks and build trust.
- The four functions—Govern, Map, Measure, Manage—provide a simple, repeatable workflow for responsible AI.
- US requirements are evolving and layered: federal guidance and executive actions set direction, while state laws—especially in California—add AI-specific obligations.

WHEN TO REVISIT YOUR AI RMF IMPLEMENTATION:

- New AI projects
- Major model updates
- Entering a regulated sector
- New state or federal guidance
- Significant incidents or near-misses

Section 2: Law, Policy, and Standards for AI Governance

2.1 The Global Regulatory Landscape

UK and International Governance Trends

1. UK uses a principles-led, pro-innovation model instead of a single AI Act.
2. Sector regulators apply 5 shared principles: safety, transparency, fairness, accountability, contestability.
3. UK AI Safety Institute tests frontier models and supports global coordination.
4. Council of Europe AI Convention: first binding international AI treaty on AI safeguards.
5. OECD AI Principles act as a widely used voluntary baseline for 40+ countries.
6. G7 Hiroshima process and bilateral deals aim for interoperability across regimes.

AI Governance Approaches at a Glance

Country / Region	Approach	Status
United Kingdom	Principles-led (no single AI Act)	In place
European Union	EU AI Act (risk-based)	In force
United States	Sectoral / agency-led	Evolving
Canada	Guidance + sectoral rules	Evolving
Australia	Principles + voluntary guardrails	In place
Japan	Guidelines + governance codes	Evolving
Singapore	Model AI Governance Framework	In place
Brazil	AI Bill (risk-based)	In progress

What you Need to Remember

UK AI governance is decentralised. Instead of a single AI Act, existing regulators interpret common principles for their own sectors, which keeps rules flexible but fragmented.

Internationally, the Council of Europe's AI Convention sets the first binding treaty on AI rights and safeguards, while the OECD AI Principles provide a shared voluntary baseline.

G7 workstreams and bilateral agreements focus on making different systems interoperable.

For organisations operating across borders, expect broadly similar values — but different regulators, processes and enforcement in each jurisdiction.

- Check which regulator oversees your AI use in each country.
- Map your systems to the 5 UK principles and OECD AI Principles.
- Design processes that can adapt to evolving international rules.

Section 2: Law, Policy, and Standards for AI Governance

2.1 The Global Regulatory Landscape

China and Other Major Jurisdictional Models

- China regulates AI through targeted rules, not one umbrella law.
- Key rules: algorithms, synthetic media / deepfakes, and generative AI services.
- Generative AI providers must register models, pass security reviews, and align content with state-defined values.
- Regulators play a direct approval and monitoring role in AI deployments.
- Brazil, Canada, India, Singapore and others are building their own AI regimes.
- Singapore's Model AI Governance Framework focuses on practical, voluntary adoption.
- Global compliance = map requirements jurisdiction by jurisdiction.

Emerging AI Regimes

China · Brazil · Canada · India · Singapore

What you Need to Remember

China's AI model is issue-specific, rapid, and state-controlled. It uses targeted rules on algorithms, synthetic media, and generative AI services rather than a single comprehensive law.

By contrast, the EU is building a comprehensive, risk-based framework, while the US remains more voluntary and sector-led.

In China, providers must register models, pass security assessments, and ensure content aligns with state-defined values—regulators play a direct approval and monitoring role.

Brazil, Canada, India, Singapore and others are moving from guidance to binding regulation, creating a more complex global landscape.

Organisations must treat each jurisdiction as a separate compliance track and build flexible, country-specific governance.

IN PRACTICE

- Create a country-by-country AI rule map
- Align internal policies to the strictest applicable standard
- Monitor fast-changing rules on algorithms, synthetic media and genAI
- Document decisions and approvals for every high-risk AI use

ISO/IEC 42001 and AI Management Systems

- **ISO/IEC 42001 is the first** international standard specifically designed for AI management systems.
- **It provides a framework for** establishing, implementing, maintaining, and continually improving AI governance.
- **The standard applies to any** organization that develops, provides, or uses AI products and services.
- **It follows the familiar Plan-Do-Check-Act (PDCA)** structure used in ISO 9001 and ISO 27001.
- **Key requirements include AI policy,** risk assessment, objective-setting, and management review.
- **Annex A contains controls specific to** AI, covering data management, system impact, and responsible use.
- **Certification against ISO/IEC 42001** signals to clients, regulators, and partners that governance is structured and verifiable.

Plan–Do–Check–Act (PDCA) Cycle

PLAN →	DO →	CHECK →	ACT
Establish AI policy, context, risks & objectives	Implement controls and operational processes	Monitor, measure & evaluate performance	Review, improve & update the AI system

What you Need to Remember

ISO/IEC 42001 is arguably the most significant development in AI governance standards in recent years — it gives organizations a concrete, auditable framework to hang their AI governance practices on, rather than relying on internal policy documents alone. It was published in December 2023 and is the world's first certifiable AI management system standard.

Unlike many AI ethics frameworks that offer principles without structure, 42001 tells you how to organize governance at the organizational level. It borrows from the well-established ISO high-level structure, so if your organization already has ISO 9001 for quality or ISO 27001 for information security, the approach will feel familiar.

The PDCA cycle means governance isn't a one-off exercise — it's designed to evolve with the technology. The standard requires you to articulate an AI policy, understand context and interested parties, assess risks specific to AI, and set measurable objectives.

Annex A is particularly practical — it gives you a library of controls covering things like data quality, system transparency, and human oversight that you can select and implement based on your risk profile.

Achieving certification doesn't just satisfy an internal checklist — it provides external, third-party verified evidence of responsible AI operation that you can show to regulators, enterprise clients, and your own board.

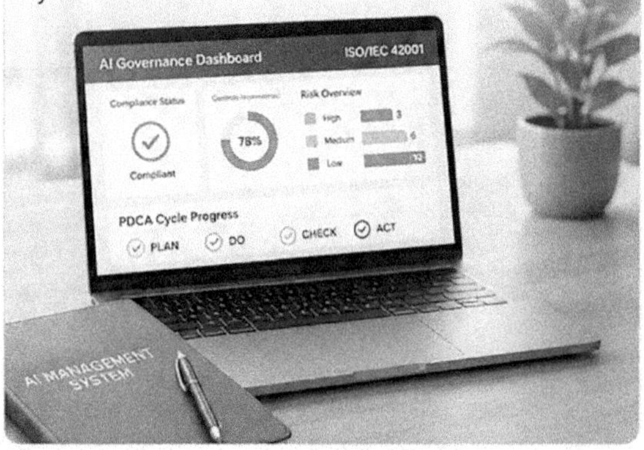

ISO/IEC 42001 at a Glance

- Published: Dec 2023
- First international certifiable AI management system standard
- Applies to any organization that develops, provides, or uses AI
- Based on ISO high-level structure (HLS)
- Provides external, verifiable assurance of responsible AI governance

Audit Trails and Decision Records

- Chronological log of AI activity so you can reconstruct what happened.
- Decision records capture inputs, system used, outputs, and any human review.
- Regulators expect evidence of what AI did, when, on what data, and who checked it.
- EU AI Act: high-risk systems must log training data, usage, and outputs for traceability.
- Useful for debugging, incident investigation, customer queries, and disputes.
- Generative AI needs extra logging: prompts, context, retrieved docs, and agent actions.

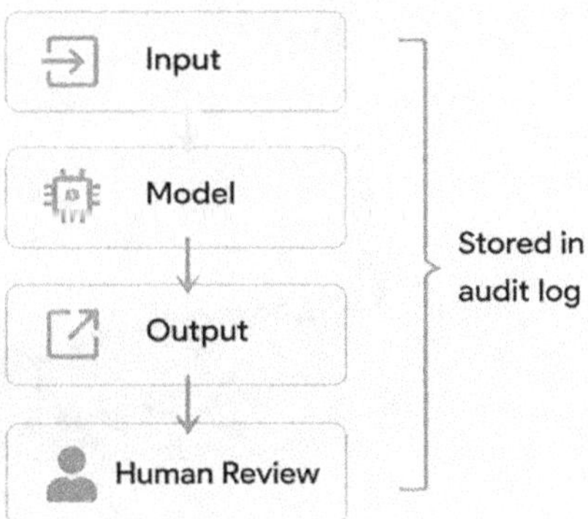

What you Need to Remember

Good governance leaves a trail of evidence. For any significant AI-assisted decision, you should be able to answer: what happened, when, using which system, under whose instruction, and with what outcome. Generative AI adds complexity because "input" can include long prompts, retrieved documents, and chains of tool calls. For high-stakes use cases, decision records must be reviewable and defensible, and EU rules make this mandatory for high-risk systems.

Start with a minimum viable record for each important interaction: use-case or process ID, system or model, date and user, short input summary, key output, and whether a human reviewed or overrode the result.

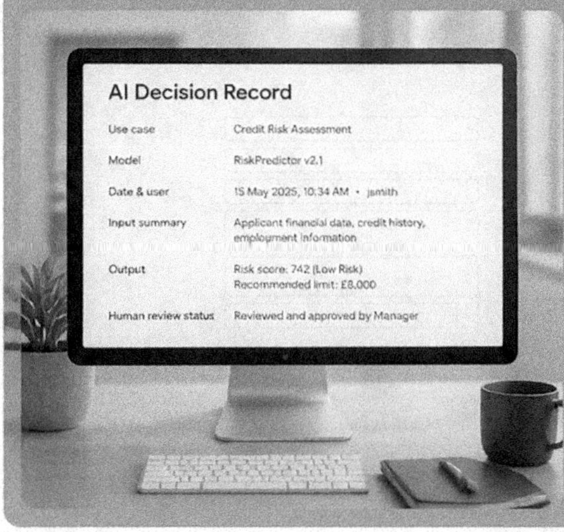

Compliance: meet EU AI Act and regulator expectations.

Operations: investigate incidents and answer client questions fast.

Learning: use logs to improve models, prompts, and processes.

2.2 Standards, Assurance, and Auditability

Internal Assurance vs External Audit

Internal assurance

Ongoing, built into day-to-day operations by your team.

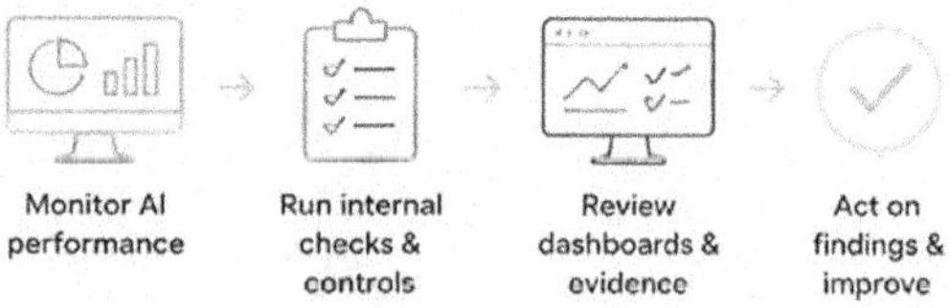

- Continuous monitoring and early issue detection.
- Owned by your team; faster, more adaptable.
- Improves systems, processes, and documentation.
- Builds accountability and a culture of quality.
- Lower cost; supports ongoing improvements.

External audit

Independent, periodic assurance by a qualified third party.

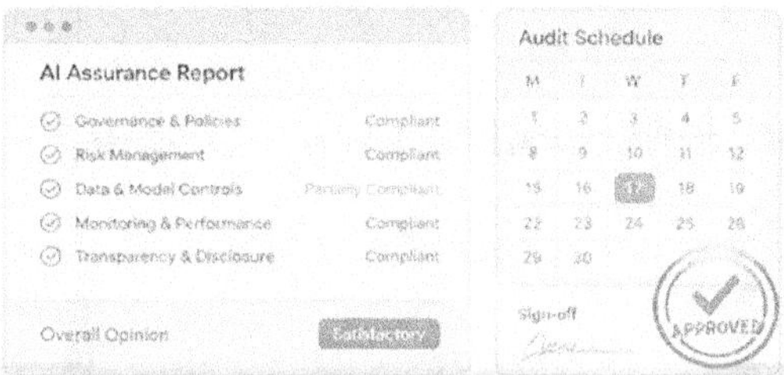

Assurance maturity: a layered approach

What you Need to Remember

Internal assurance is continuous and owned by your team. It helps you monitor AI systems, catch issues early, and drive ongoing improvement.

External audit provides independent, periodic validation that your AI governance, controls, and performance meet required standards and stakeholder expectations.

First-party, second-party, and third-party assurance build on each other—maturity grows as you add independent perspectives.

Use internal assurance for agility and improvement, and external audit for credibility and trust. Together, they deliver stronger AI risk management and confident decision-making.

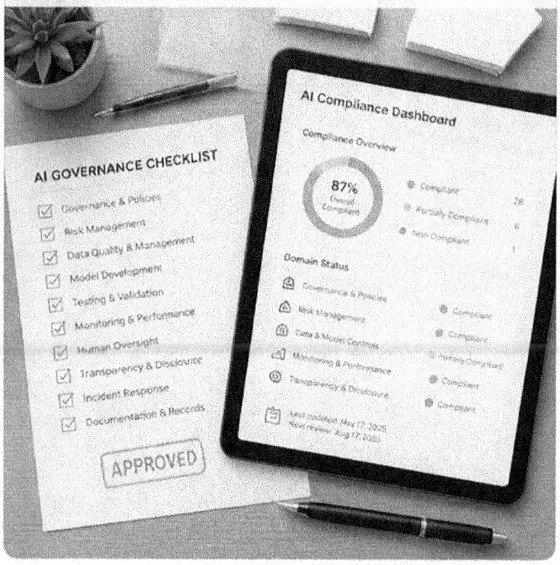

When to rely on internal assurance

- Daily monitoring and control checks
- Early detection of issues
- Process improvement and agility

When to bring in external audit

- Compliance and regulatory needs
- Stakeholder and investor assurance
- Major changes or high-risk areas

Questions to ask your auditor

- What standards will you assess?
- What's in scope—and out of scope?
- How will findings be reported and followed up?

Evidence Packs for Regulators, Clients and Boards

What is an evidence pack?

- A structured set of documents and records that demonstrate responsible AI.
- Used to show compliance, manage risk, and build trust.

Tailor to the audience

- Regulators: risk class, controls, testing, incidents.
- Enterprise clients: data safety, contracts, access.
- Boards: risk posture, key issues, incidents.

Core components

- AI policy
- Risk register
- Use-case register
- Audit logs
- Incident & bias reports
- Training & oversight records

Good practice

- Living document
- Regular updates
- Version control
- Named owner

Evidence Pack Index + New Pack

System	Audience	Last updated	Owner
Loan Underwriting AI	Regulators	13 May 2025	R. Patel
Fraud Detection AI	Enterprise Clients	12 May 2025	J. Wong
Customer Support AI	Boards	09 May 2025	M. Ibrahim
Marketing Content AI	Enterprise Clients	07 May 2025	S. Lee
Code Assistant AI	Boards	05 May 2025	T. Morgan

View all evidence packs

What you Need to Remember

Evidence packs exist to prove your organisation is building and using AI responsibly.

Different audiences care about different proof. Regulators want to see risk class, controls, testing, and incidents. Enterprise clients want data safety, contractual commitments, and access rights. Boards want a clear view of overall risk posture, key issues, and incidents that matter most.

Build and version your packs proactively. Keep them structured, up to date, and easy to navigate so you can respond quickly to requests and audits.

Strong evidence practices signal governance maturity—and they let you show what your governance looked like at a point in time.

Define audience first

Keep one source of truth

Capture changes as they happen

Acceptable Use Policies for AI Tools

1. What an AUP does
Sets clear expectations for safe and responsible use of AI tools.

2. Typical approved uses
Drafting, summarising, research, and internal analysis to boost productivity.

3. Typical prohibited uses
Sharing confidential information, creating misleading content, or bypassing security.

4. Escalation routes
Know who to contact if you're unsure about a use or outcome.

5. Good AUPs are
Short, specific, and written in plain language for quick understanding.

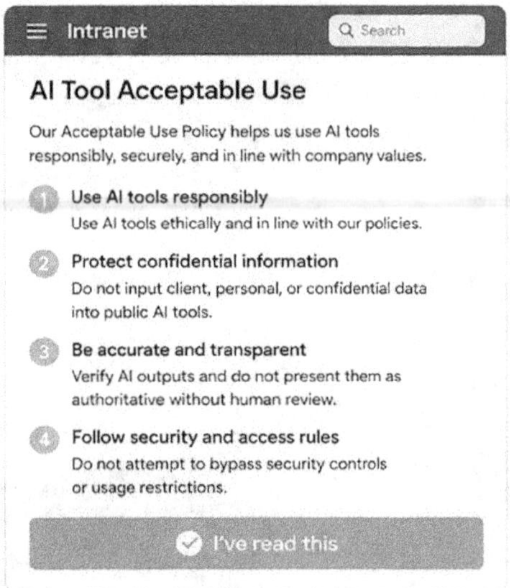

What you Need to Remember

An Acceptable Use Policy (AUP) is the front door of AI governance. It sets clear expectations so everyone can use AI tools with confidence and consistency.

Approved uses focus on everyday productivity tasks—drafting content, summarising information, research, and internal analysis—to save time and improve quality.

Prohibited uses target real risks, such as entering client or sensitive data into public AI tools, producing misleading or unverified content, or attempting to bypass security.

Escalation pathways ensure you don't have to guess. When unsure, escalate early to the right people to protect you, your team, and our clients.

The best AUPs are short, written in plain language, and focused on action—helping people understand what to do, what to avoid, and where to get help.

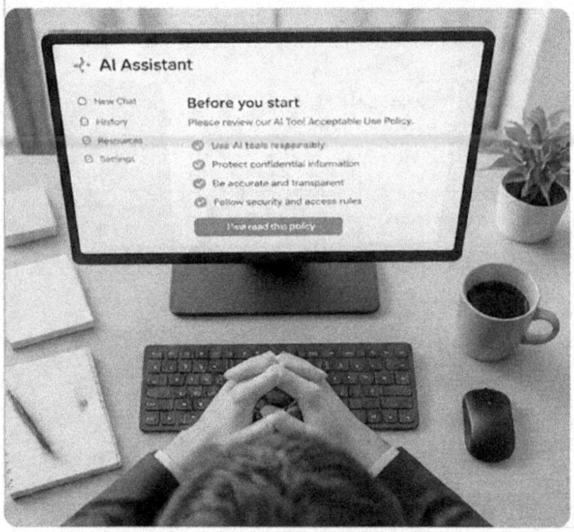

Check if my use case is allowed	Flag a potential policy breach	Summarise this policy for my team	Suggest clearer wording for a policy rule

Drafting an Acceptable Use Policy — Key Components

1. Scope
Which tools, which users, which contexts.

2. Approved use cases
Everyday tasks and 'safe to try' examples.

3. Prohibited use cases
High-risk actions and why they're blocked.

4. Data handling rules
What data can / cannot go into AI tools.

5. Ownership & review
Who owns outputs and keeps the policy current.

Draft AUP Checklist

- Define scope
- List approved tasks
- Flag red lines
- Set data rules

What you Need to Remember

- Start with scope: name the AI tools and who can use them.
- Give concrete approved examples so staff can decide quickly.
- Explain the 'why' behind prohibited uses to encourage buy-in.
- Be explicit about sensitive data that must stay out of external models.
- Assign an owner and review cycle so the policy keeps pace with AI change.

When to update your AUP
New AI tools rolled out

Change in data or privacy rules

Incidents or near-misses

Section 2: Law, Policy, and Standards for AI Governance

2.3 Internal AI Policy Design

Model and Vendor Approval Policies

- Risk varies by tool – approvals keep evaluation consistent.
- Check where data is processed, who can see it, and how long it's kept.
- Enterprise versions of tools (e.g. ChatGPT, Claude, Copilot) usually give stronger data protections.
- Decisions should involve IT, security, legal and the business owner.
- An approved tools list cuts shadow AI and gives staff safe choices.

AI Tool Request

In Review

Tool name	Example AI Tool
Purpose	Marketing content generation
Data location	AWS – Europe (Frankfurt)
Access controls	SSO, Role-based access, MFA
Retention	30 days
Data used for training	No
Vendor security certifications	ISO 27001, SOC 2 Type II
Business justification	Improve content creation speed and quality.
Requested by	Marketing Team
Approval status	In Review
Approvers	IT, Sec, Legal, Biz
Notes	Security review in progress.

What you Need to Remember

- Staff are already using AI; policies decide whether they use approved tools.
- A vendor approval process creates a gateway so tools are assessed before wide adoption.
- Data processing terms are critical; consumer tiers may train on inputs and lack controls.
- Enterprise offerings like ChatGPT Enterprise, Claude for Enterprise and Microsoft 365 Copilot are built for business data but still need review.
- Bringing IT, security, legal and the requesting team together avoids blind spots and ends with a published approved tools list everyone can follow.

Check before you sign up | Use enterprise tiers where possible | Log new tool requests | Refer to the approved tools list

Evaluating AI Tools for Approval — A Practical Framework

Data residency
Check where data is stored and processed, and whether locations meet your regulatory requirements.

Training & retention
Confirm if your prompts and files are used to train models and how long any data is retained.

Access controls
Look for SSO, role-based access, audit logs, and admin tools to restrict data scope.

Vendor transparency
Prefer vendors who publish model documentation, safety evaluations, and clear usage policies.

Contractual terms
Ensure terms cover data processing, confidentiality, IP ownership, and liability in line with your policies.

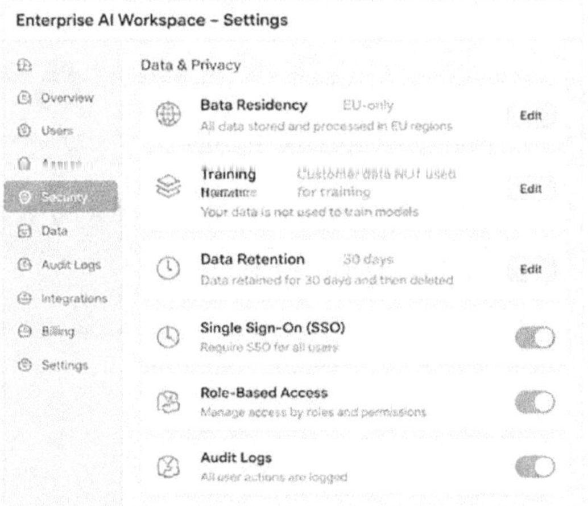

What you Need to Remember

Data residency is the first approval filter. Verify where data is stored and processed and ensure it meets GDPR and any sector-specific regulatory requirements.

Enterprise plans often exclude training on customer data, but you must confirm this explicitly and ensure it is written into the contract.

Robust access controls and vendor transparency—such as clear usage policies and model cards—are essential for ongoing governance and risk management.

Legal review of DPAs, liability, and IP terms is the final gate before sign-off to ensure your organisation is protected.

QUICK APPROVAL CHECKLIST

1. Confirm data locations + residency fit.
2. Lock in training, retention, and access in the contract.
3. Get sign-off from security, privacy, and legal.

Employee Guidance for Prompting and Review

- Use prompting guidance to get useful outputs while avoiding compliance and quality risks.
- Never include personal data, confidential details, or client identifiers in prompts.
- Treat AI output as a draft — always check facts, figures, and tone before use.
- Apply a consistent rule for when and how AI assistance is disclosed in external documents.
- Tailor guidance by role: marketers, lawyers, and analysts each face different risks.

What you Need to Remember

Prompt rules turn AI governance into everyday behaviour — every prompt should protect data and reputation.

Minimise data in prompts and keep client names, personal information, and sensitive figures out of external tools.

Because AI can sound confident but be wrong, build habits of review, sensible disclosure of AI use, and role-specific checklists.

Always review	Protect data	Disclose AI use	Role-specific rules

Building a Prompting and Review Culture

Teach prompting as a skill
Short, focused sessions with worked examples, not one-off documents.

Standard templates
Shared prompt libraries for common tasks reduce risky improvisation.

Review checklists
Simple, repeatable checks for accuracy, tone, data sources and disclosure.

Positive framing
Position review as quality assurance and support, not AI distrust.

Champions & peer learning
Early adopters share good prompts and feedback in team settings.

Approved Prompt Library

What you Need to Remember

Publishing guidance is not the same as building culture. Treat prompting like any other core skill: show examples, explain patterns, and give feedback so behaviour becomes consistent.

Approved prompt libraries raise the quality floor for high-impact workflows.

Review checklists turn 'be careful' into specific steps: verify data and sources, check tone and bias, confirm policy alignment and AI disclosure.

Present review as part of doing great work, not as AI scepticism.

Visible peer champions who share prompts, run quick huddles and celebrate good use of AI make the culture real.

When to Refresh Prompts & Checks

New use case	Higher risk decision	Team feedback	Policy or tool change

Policy Refresh Cycles

- AI tools evolve faster than traditional software — policy must keep pace.
- Use trigger-based reviews for major product changes, incidents, or new regulations.
- Keep a scheduled AI policy review every 6–12 months.
- Policy owners track vendor release notes and regulatory updates as part of their role.
- Apply version control and notify staff so everyone uses the current policy.

AI Policy Governance Dashboard

Tool	Last Major Update	Policy Status	Status
AI Assistant	May 15, 2025	Up to date	Current
Content Generator	Apr 28, 2025	Review due	Review
Image Creator	May 1, 2025	Under review	Review
Data Analyser	Mar 30, 2025	Out of date	Overdue
Transcription Tool	Feb 18, 2025	Out of date	Overdue

Last updated: May 20, 2025 Next review cycle: Nov 20, 2025

AI capabilities can leap from 'drafting and summarisation' to autonomous actions overnight. Each big feature release can open a policy gap if approvals don't match what the tool can now do.

Combine trigger-based reviews (after major product updates, incidents, or new guidance) with a regular review cycle. Treat vendor release notes as inputs to governance, not just product news.

When policies change, governance owns communication: if staff are following an out-of-date policy, that's a process failure, not a people failure.

Step 1
Monitor: product updates, incidents, regulations.
→
Step 2
Decide: assess risk and update policy if needed.
→
Step 3
Communicate: publish new version and brief teams.

Maintaining a Living Policy Framework

- Assign an owner, next-review date, and change log to every AI policy.
- Keep a central policy register showing current, in-review, and overdue documents.
- Make it obvious where staff find the latest version and who to ask for help.
- Plan regular policy touchpoints – not just update emails – so governance stays visible.
- Use sunset dates to retire rules when tools or processes are replaced.

AI Policy Register

Policy Title	Owner	Last Review	Next Review	Status
AI Acceptable Use Policy	Alex Morgan	15 Jan 2025	15 Jul 2025	Current
Data Privacy & Protection in AI Systems	Priya Shah	22 Dec 2024	22 Jun 2025	Current
Responsible AI Principles	Jordan Lee	10 Feb 2025	10 Aug 2025	Current
AI Model Risk Management	Sam Patel	05 Nov 2024	05 May 2025	Review due
Vendor & Third-Party AI Governance	Taylor Kim	18 Oct 2024	18 Apr 2025	Overdue
AI Incident Response Plan	Casey Reed	12 Sep 2024	12 Mar 2025	Overdue
AI Training & Awareness	Morgan Ellis	07 Jan 2025	07 Jul 2025	Current

What you Need to Remember

Strong AI governance depends on operational hygiene. Without it, even the best-written policies quickly become out of date and too hard to trust.

Every AI policy must clearly show who owns it, when it was last reviewed, when it's due next, and the history of changes.

A simple policy register gives you a single source of truth so your team can see what's current, what needs review, and what's overdue.

Communicate updates and upcoming reviews in the normal flow of work so accountability becomes routine.

Use sunset clauses to retire policies when the tools or processes they cover are replaced – outdated rules create risk.

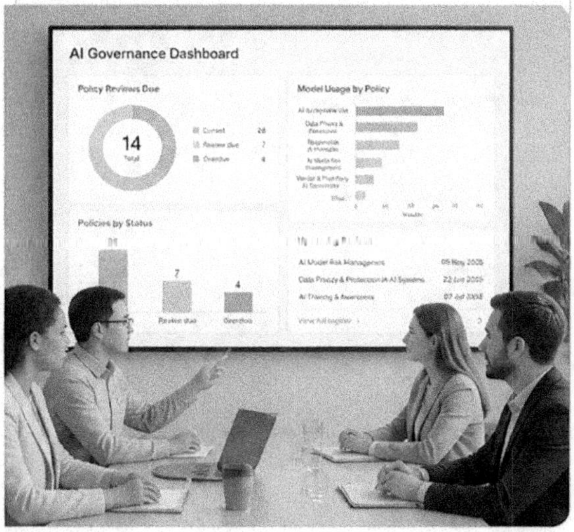

- Check the owner
- Check the review date
- Check the status in the register

Buying AI Responsibly

- Most AI in your organization comes from third-party vendors, not in-house builds.
- Procurement is a primary governance control point — what you buy shapes what you can govern.
- Apply due diligence to platforms, APIs, embedded AI, and copilot features.
- Ask: What happens to our data? Who is liable for outputs? What controls do we get?
- Getting procurement right is far cheaper than fixing issues after deployment.

AI Vendor Due Diligence

Category	Vendor A	Vendor B	Vendor C	Status
Data Handling Data use, retention & training	✓	–	✗	Good
Liability & Indemnity Liability limits & indmnnification	✓	✗	–	Review
Admin Controls Access, roles & security settings	✓	✓	–	Good
Transparency Model info, disclosures & documentation	–	✗	✓	High Risk

Overall recommendation: Review Required   Last updated: May 20, 2025

What you Need to Remember

Most enterprise AI is bought from vendors, so your buying decisions are one of the most powerful governance levers.

Treat AI tools like any other high-risk technology purchase — use structured due diligence and risk assessment before rollout.

Clarify how data will be used, who is responsible for harmful outputs, and what administrative controls you will have before you commit.

Before You Sign
Standard AI due-diligence checklist.

Red Flag Signals
Unclear data use or shared liability.

Document & Monitor
Keep a vendor risk log & review annually.

Due Diligence for Platforms, Copilots, and Embedded AI

- List every AI feature in the product – including hidden or 'smart' options that aren't sold as AI.
- Check data processing terms: who sees prompts and files, where they're processed, and for what purpose.
- Confirm whether your data can be used to train or fine-tune the vendor's models.
- Prefer enterprise or business tiers – consumer plans often have weaker governance controls.
- Map each AI component to your internal risk category before approving deployment.

AI Vendor Assessment

Search vendors...

Product	AI Features	Data Use	Tier	Risk Category
Product Alpha	Chat, Summary, Smart Search	No training use. Encrypted in transit & at rest.	Enterprise	Low
Product Beta	Copilot, Code Assist, Insights	May use content to improve models.	Business	Medium
Product Gamma	AI Extract, Auto Classify	Used for training and fine-tuning.	Pro	High
Product Delta	Meeting Notes, Transcription	No training use. EU data region.	Enterprise	Low
Product Epsilon	AI Writer, Image Gen	May use data to improve models.	Standard	Medium

Last updated: Today, 09.30 — Low · Medium · High

What you Need to Remember

Successful AI procurement starts with visibility. Identify every AI capability in the product—including embedded or "smart" features that may not be marketed as AI. Focus due diligence on how data is processed, who can access it, whether it can be used for training or fine-tuning, and where processing takes place to meet your data sovereignty and compliance requirements.

Map each AI use to your organisation's risk framework before approving deployment. Understand the impact on people, decisions, and sensitive data, then apply proportionate controls, contractual safeguards, and ongoing monitoring. When in doubt, pause, ask questions, and escalate.

- Unclear data training terms
- Cross-border data transfers
- High-stakes decisions (hiring, credit, safety)
- Vendors unwilling to sign governance addendum

Vendor Transparency and Control Expectations

Security posture
Certifications, pen tests, breach alerts.

Data retention
How long prompts, outputs, and files are stored.

Audit logs
Visibility into what was sent to and from the AI.

Admin controls
Ability to configure, restrict, or disable features.

Transparency & model changes
Notifications when models or policies change.

What you Need to Remember

Evaluate AI vendors for transparency and control before adoption. Confirm they maintain strong security certifications, conduct regular pen tests, and have clear breach notification processes with defined timelines.

Understand data retention defaults and what you can configure. Know how long prompts, outputs, and uploaded files are stored, where data resides, and how deletion requests are handled.

Ensure comprehensive audit logs are available for all interactions, including what was sent to and received from the AI. Logs should be exportable, searchable, and retained to meet your regulatory and compliance requirements.

Verify that admin controls let you configure, restrict, or disable features like file uploads or external connectors. Confirm you'll be notified when models or policies change so your governance stays effective in practice.

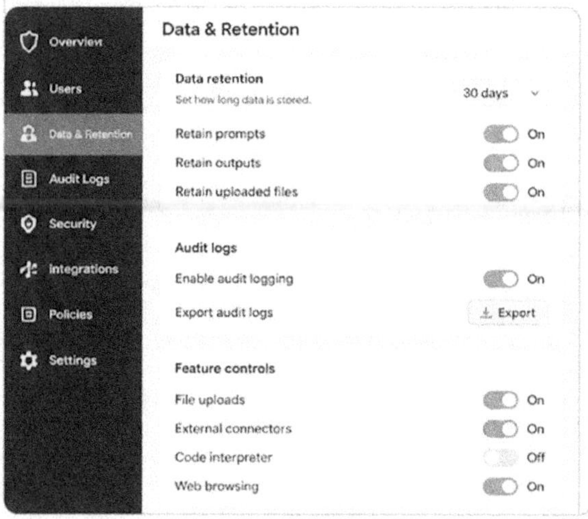

Document vendor answers and map them to your policies.

Classify vendors by risk level before rollout.

Bake transparency and control commitments into contracts.

Open-Source vs Proprietary Models

1. Proprietary models:
Vendor support, SLAs, managed updates.

2. Open-source models:
More control, need internal capability.

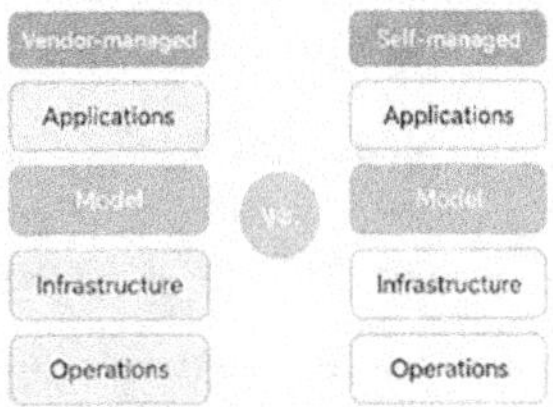

3. Open-source still needs:
Security, access controls, and monitoring.

4. Proprietary risk:
Vendor lock-in and opaque internals.

5. Governance focus:
Choose based on fit to capability and risk profile.

What you Need to Remember

Neither open-source nor proprietary models are inherently more governable. Each brings trade-offs that affect control, risk, and operational responsibility.

Proprietary models offer vendor support, SLA-backed service, and predictable updates—but they create dependence on the vendor and limited visibility into internal workings.

Open-source models give you more control and flexibility—yet they require strong internal capability to enforce security, manage access, and monitor systems continuously.

The right choice depends on your organization's capability, resources, and risk tolerance. Align the model you choose with the governance you can deliver.

Questions to Ask Vendors
Transparency, audit logs, update policy.

Checks for Self-Hosted Models
Access control, patching, incident response.

When to Revisit Your Model Choice
Capability changes, new regulations, major incidents.

Shared Responsibility in AI Ecosystems

Responsibility is layered
Safe and effective AI use depends on everyone in the ecosystem — model provider, platform vendor, your organization, and the end user.

Vendors set the foundation
Model providers and platform vendors are responsible for model safety, security, infrastructure, and terms of use.

Organizations own the context
Your organization is responsible for use-case fit, data governance, access controls, monitoring, and acceptable use policies.

Users drive day-to-day use
End users are responsible for the prompts they write, the outputs they rely on, and how they use AI in their work.

Gaps create governance risk
Failures happen when each party assumes someone else is covering the risk.

Who is Responsible for What?

Responsibility Area	Model Provider	Platform Vendor	Your Organization	End User
Model safety & alignment	✓			
Security & infrastructure	✓	✓		
Data governance & privacy		✓	✓	
Use-case fit & risk management			✓	
Access controls & monitoring			✓	
Terms, policies & compliance	✓	✓	✓	
Prompting & safe use				✓
Review & act on outputs			✓	✓

What you Need to Remember

AI ecosystems are built on shared responsibility. No single party controls every risk.

Model providers design and train models and work to make them safe and aligned. They set guardrails, release updates, and define terms.

Platform vendors run the services that deliver models— handling uptime, security, access, and platform-level controls.

Your organization decides how AI is used. You assess use cases, protect data, set policies, manage access, monitor behaviour, and ensure compliance.

End users interact with AI every day. They must prompt responsibly, validate outputs, respect policies, and escalate issues.

Breakdowns occur when one layer assumes another has it covered. Strong outcomes come from clear roles, good communication, and continuous oversight across the full chain.

- Clarify who owns each risk
- Document roles in policies
- Train users to spot gaps
- Review regularly

SECTION 3

Data, Security, and Privacy for AI Systems

In this section, we look at the data, security and privacy dimensions of AI, the areas where organisations make some of their most common unforced errors. Many incidents stem not from malice or sophisticated attacks, but from someone failing to ask what kind of data they are handling, where it is going, who can access it, and what happens to it afterwards.

We start with data governance foundations: classification into tiers, from public to highly confidential; minimisation, giving the model only what it needs; retention, deletion and traceability; and cross-border sovereignty questions under GDPR, since AI often runs on globally distributed infrastructure. We also look at why account type and configuration matter. Consumer and enterprise AI services can have very different arrangements for storing prompts, using data for training, and providing administrative controls. Outputs need governance too: organisations should be able to trace what was submitted, by whom, what the AI returned, and how that output was subsequently used.

We then examine AI-specific security threats: prompt injection and instruction hijacking that manipulate the model's context; silent data leakage, where an output simply contains something it should not; tool misuse and agent overreach once AI moves from conversation to action; and identity and access design, a recurring failure point. Agents capable of accessing files, systems or business processes should have their own scoped identities and permissions rather than inheriting broad or administrative privileges.

Privacy and personal data receive detailed treatment: personal information entering systems innocently through prompts, documents and connected data sources; consent and lawful basis under GDPR; employee monitoring through workplace

AI; and Data Protection Impact Assessments as a structured judgement rather than a checkbox. The aim is to recognise privacy risk before information has already travelled somewhere it should not.

The section closes on content integrity: data lineage and source traceability; output verification and citation discipline to counter confident hallucinations, including plausible fabrications such as non-existent legal cases; and deepfakes and synthetic media as a mainstream business risk. We also examine watermarking, metadata and provenance signals, whose limitations mean they can support verification but cannot replace it.

Taken together, these controls provide a practical foundation for handling AI data securely, protecting privacy, and maintaining confidence in both what goes into an AI system and what comes back out.

Data Classification for AI Use

Public
Safe for any AI prompt – content already public (e.g. website, press release).

Internal
Operational but non-public – strip out identifiers and sensitive detail before prompting.

Confidential
Commercially sensitive – only use in approved tools with strong access controls.

Restricted
Highest-risk data (personal, health, legal, credentials) – almost never goes into prompts.

What you Need to Remember

Most AI misuse isn't malicious – it happens because people paste data into tools without thinking about what kind of data it is.

The four-tier model (Public, Internal, Confidential, Restricted) maps to most enterprise policies and should be your default lens before every prompt.

Classification has to happen first: once data is in an external AI system, the exposure has already happened.

Before you prompt

1. Identify the document or data →
2. Assign a classification →
3. Decide: safe to use, redact, or don't use

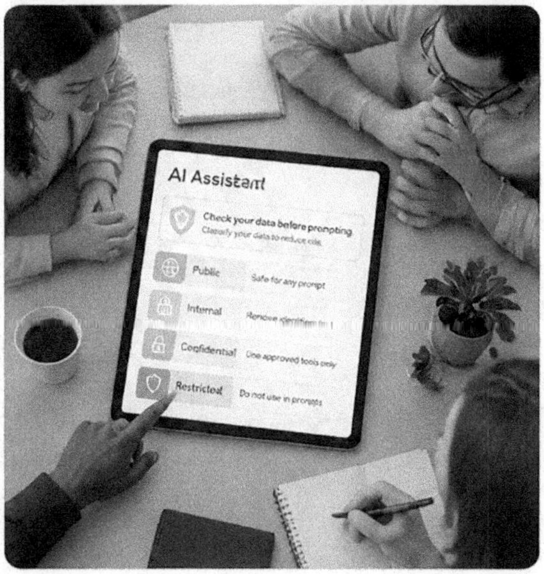

Quick Checks Before You Paste into AI

- Does it include personal data?
- Would I share this with a competitor?
- Is there a safer internal tool?
- Can I anonymise or summarise it first?
- Am I allowed to store this in the AI tool?

Data Minimization in Prompts and Workflows

- Share only the data the AI genuinely needs for the task.
- Over-sharing is the most common governance failure in daily AI use.
- Remove names, IDs, and personal identifiers before uploading documents.
- Use synthetic or anonymised examples when testing prompts or workflows.
- In automated pipelines, filter sensitive fields before data reaches the model.
- Less data in means less data at risk — minimisation is a powerful control.

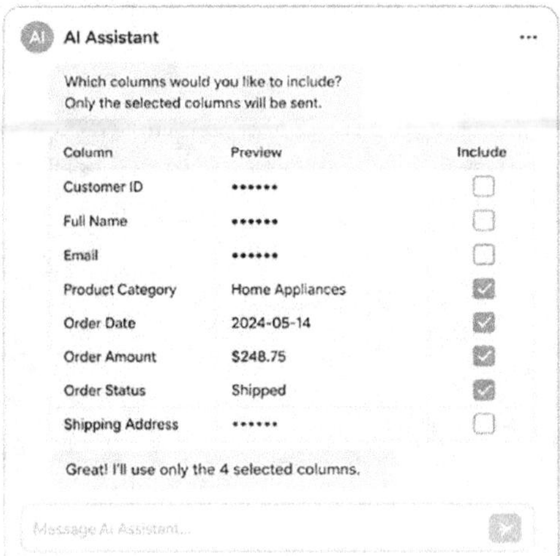

What you Need to Remember

Data minimisation is a long-standing privacy principle that fits perfectly within AI governance: collect, share, and use only what is necessary.

Uploading whole files or full email threads is unnecessary risk when the AI only needs a slice of the information to complete the task.

Make it a habit to strip out personal identifiers and sensitive details before sharing with any AI tool — it's a fast and effective way to reduce risk.

Synthetic data is ideal for testing prompts and workflows without exposing real information. In automated pipelines, filtering should happen before the AI model, not after.

Always ask: does the AI actually need this piece of data?

- Filter at source
- Remove identifiers
- Use synthetic data
- Set sharing rules
- Ask if it's needed

Retention, Deletion, and Traceability

- Prompts may leave your control once sent to an AI service.
- Each tool (ChatGPT, Copilot, Claude, etc.) handles retention and training use differently.
- Default settings and account type strongly affect how long data is kept and how it's used.
- Enterprise accounts usually offer stricter retention, privacy, and training-use controls.
- AI outputs are records too and must be stored and managed.
- Governance requires logs of who submitted what, when, and what the AI returned.

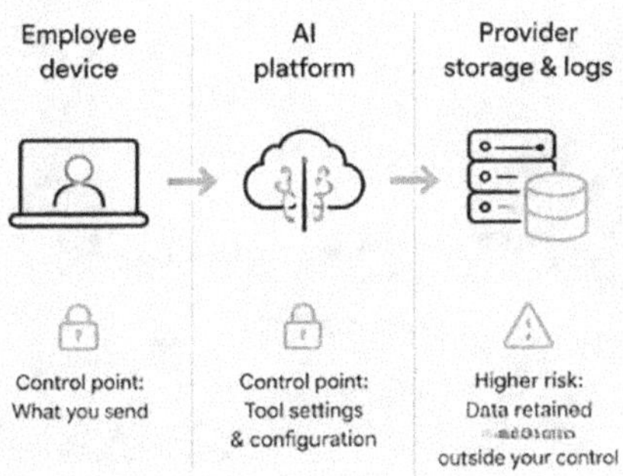

What you Need to Remember

Consumer AI accounts often use your prompts and outputs to improve their models by default, while enterprise accounts may not.

Contracts and configuration—such as opting out of training use, setting retention periods, and defining data locations—are real governance controls.

AI-generated documents are business records. Apply versioning, retention rules, and traceability so you can explain what was produced, when, by whom, and under which rules.

- Standardise approved AI accounts and settings
- Enable logging for prompts and outputs
- Define retention rules for AI-generated records

Section 3: Data, Security, and Privacy for AI Systems

3.1 Data Governance for Generative AI

Cross-Border and Sovereignty Issues

- AI services process data on infrastructure in multiple countries.
- Data residency rules keep some data in specific jurisdictions.
- GDPR limits transfers of personal data outside the EEA without safeguards.
- Sector rules (health, finance, government) can be stricter.
- Cloud regions and data processing agreements are key controls.
- Organizations must verify AI vendor data residency commitments.

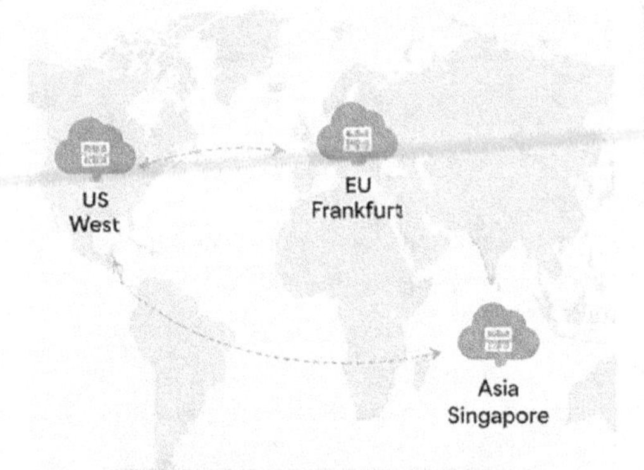

What you Need to Remember

AI tools run on global cloud infrastructure. Your data may be stored or processed in locations you didn't choose or even know about.

When data is regulated—such as personal, health, government, or financial data—where it is physically processed becomes a legal issue, not just a technical detail.

Laws like the GDPR and other sector or sovereignty rules restrict transfers of data across borders unless strict conditions or safeguards are met.

Major AI vendors offer regional hosting and data processing agreements, but these protections only apply if you purchase the right tier and configure services correctly.

Don't assume compliance. Verify, configure, and document your vendor's data residency commitments and keep evidence in your AI governance records.

Next steps

- Map regulated data and locations
- Review AI vendor contracts and regions
- Record decisions in your AI register

Prompt Injection and Instruction Hijacking

Prompt injection = malicious instructions hidden in content the model reads.

Models can't reliably tell trusted instructions from injected ones.

Direct attacks: prompts that try to override system rules.

Indirect attacks: hostile text buried in docs, sites, or data feeds.

Successful attacks change behaviour, leak secrets, or trigger unsafe actions.

Agentic AIs amplify risk because they can act on hijacked instructions.

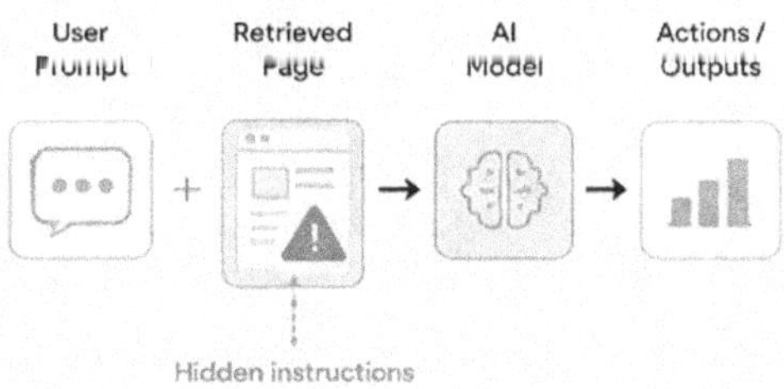

What you Need to Remember

LLMs follow whatever is in their context window. Attackers try to poison that context.

Prompt injection can be direct—written to override rules—or indirect—hidden inside documents, websites, or data feeds that the model retrieves and reads.

When tools and systems are connected, hijacked instructions can lead to real-world actions, data exposure, or policy violations. The stakes are higher.

Managing what models can read and what they can do is a governance responsibility, not just a vendor fix.

- Limit model permissions
- Validate retrieved content
- Log and monitor AI actions
- Train staff to spot risky prompts

Data Leakage and Sensitive Output Risk

- Models can resurface sensitive training or retrieved content.
- Well-crafted prompts may elicit confidential information.
- System prompts, retrieval results, and memory are leakage surfaces.
- Externally shared outputs can expose internal data silently.
- Leakage can be accidental or driven by hostile prompt attacks.
- Data classification and output review are your main controls.

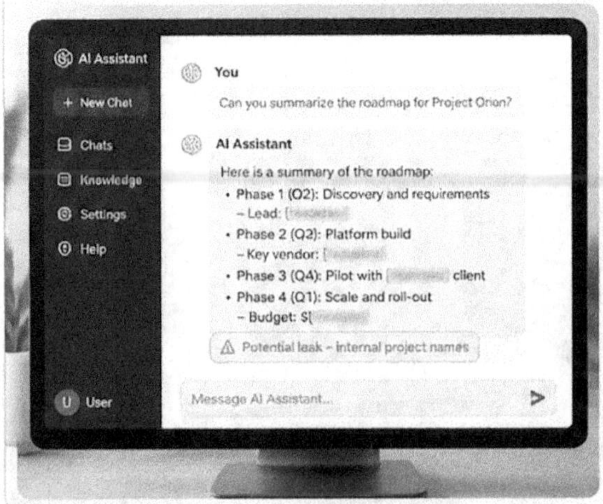

What you Need to Remember

AI data leakage isn't like a logged database breach—models can quote anything in their context window.

RAG and memory systems can surface confidential content you never intended to reveal.

Shared outputs can unintentionally expose strategy, personnel, clients, or financial data.

Attackers can probe models to reconstruct documents and extract sensitive details.

Strong defences focus on keeping sensitive data out of the prompt pipeline and reviewing outputs before they leave your organisation.

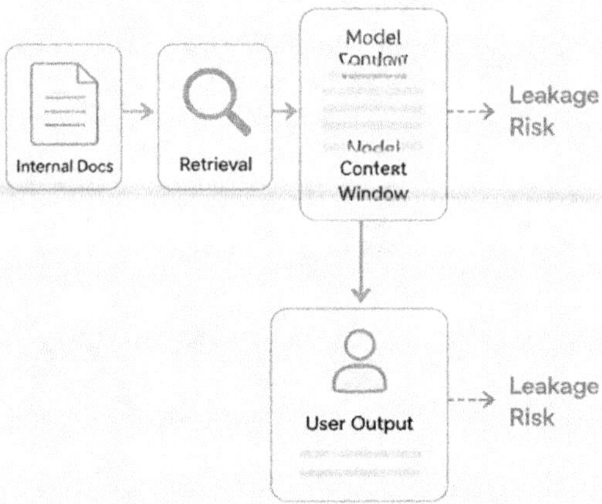

QUICK SAFEGUARDS

- Block highly sensitive data from training & RAG corpora.
- Classify prompts & responses; flag likely confidential terms.
- Require human review before sharing externally.

Tool Misuse and Agent Overreach

- Agentic tools can browse, read files, send emails, and call APIs.
- Overreach = actions that go beyond what the task actually required.
- One compromised instruction can trigger a long chain of real-world actions.
- Prompt injection, vague goals, and loose scope often drive tool misuse.
- Treat deletions, sent messages, and submitted forms as 'irreversible'.
- Limit each agent to the minimum tools needed to shrink the blast radius.

AI Agent Tool Access Panel

Configure which tools this agent can use.

Tool	Description	Access
Web Browsing	Search and browse the internet.	Off
File Access	Read and analyze files and folders.	On
Email	Send and read emails.	Off
Payments	Initiate payments and transfers.	Off

Only enable the tools this agent truly needs.

What you Need to Remember

Once AI moves from chat to action, the governance stakes rise sharply. Actions persist after the session ends, and their impact can be lasting.

Overreach doesn't require a hacker. Broad goals plus wide tool access means the system may simply do more than you intended.

Injected instructions inside retrieved documents can fully redirect the task. The model follows the latest instructions it sees, not your original intent.

Irreversible actions demand explicit human approval. The core design rule is simple: minimum viable tooling.

Ask: What can this agent touch?

Block: Irreversible actions by default.

Require: Human sign-off for high-impact steps.

Identity, Access, and Permission Design

- Design AI with least-privilege access – only what it genuinely needs.
- Don't let agents inherit the full permissions of the person who set them up.
- Give AI systems their own identities so actions are auditable.
- Scope permissions to each task, not to the requester's job role.
- Use just-in-time access for sensitive steps, then expire it.
- Review and remove unused AI permissions regularly as workflows change.

DIFFERENT ACCESS. DIFFERENT RISK.

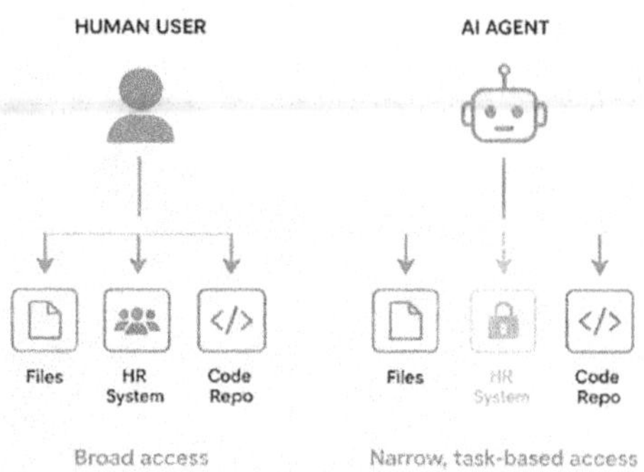

What you Need to Remember

Giving an AI agent the same powerful account you use is convenient—but unsafe. Any prompt injection or misuse can act with those admin rights.

Instead, treat every AI as its own user with narrowly scoped, task-based permissions.

That way audit logs clearly show what the AI did versus the human, and a coding agent never sees HR data it doesn't need.

Because access tends to grow and rarely shrinks, schedule regular permission reviews to remove anything no longer required.

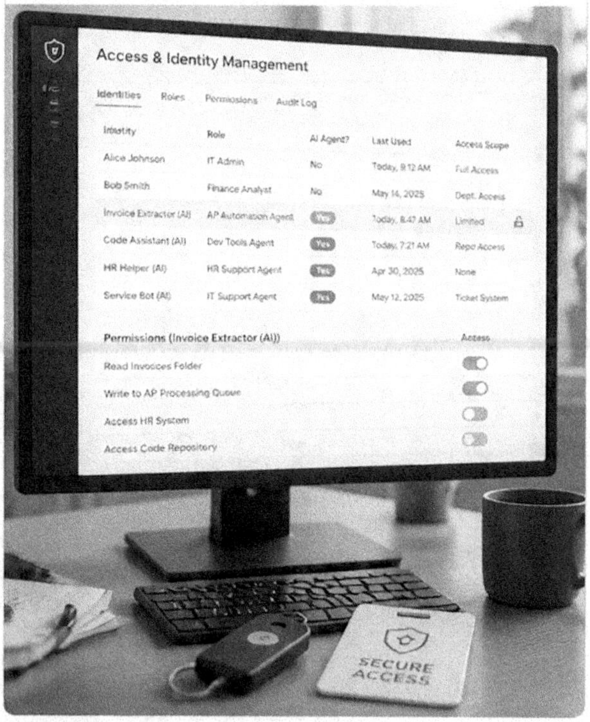

- Start with least privilege
- Review AI access regularly
- Audit AI activity separately from humans

Section 3: Data, Security, and Privacy for AI Systems

3.3 Privacy and Personal Data in AI Operations

Privacy and Personal Data in AI Operations

AI tools routinely handle personal data — often without people realising.

Privacy governance is not just legal compliance — it's how you run AI safely day to day.

Focus on four questions: what data goes in, what legal basis you rely on, how outcomes impact people, and what checks you must document.

We'll apply this to prompts, file uploads, consent, workplace monitoring, and privacy impact assessments.

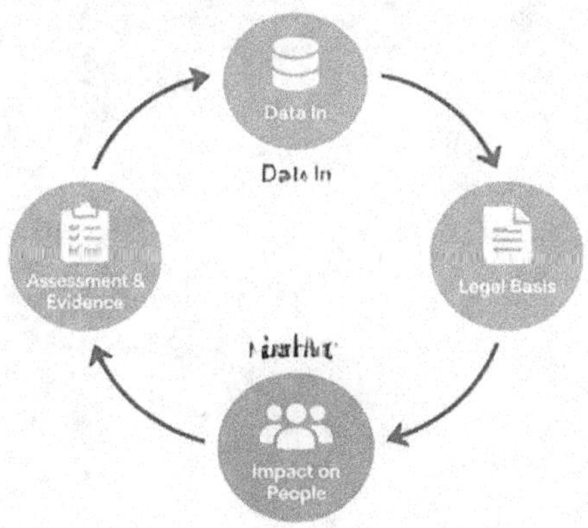

What you Need to Remember

Personal data and AI are tightly linked — and errors here create real legal, ethical, and reputational risk.

Most issues don't come from the AI model itself, but from how teams feed in identifiable data and act on the outputs.

Before using personal data, be clear on why it's needed, what lawful basis you rely on, and how you'll respect people's rights.

Pay special attention to employee data and monitoring — expectations of fairness and transparency are higher.

Use privacy impact assessments to document risks and controls before rolling out AI into everyday workflows.

Before you prompt

- Strip out names and IDs.
- Use synthetic examples where possible.

If you use real data

- Confirm lawful basis.
- Limit who can access outputs.

Build the habit

- Log high-risk prompts.
- Escalate grey areas to privacy or legal.

Personal Data in Prompts and Uploads

1. People paste names, emails, salaries, health info, and customer details into prompts.

Name	Email	Salary	Health Plan	Customer ID
[illegible]	jane.doe@acme.com	$98,750	Gold	C-48291
[illegible]	mike.smith@acme.com	$87,200	Silver	C-48292
[illegible]	sara.lee@acme.com	$105,300	Gold	C-48293

2. Uploading full files (CSVs, decks, docs) often exposes more data than you realise.

3. Some consumer AI tools reuse prompt data for training if enterprise controls aren't enabled.

4. Typical mistakes: full datasets instead of samples, real names in demos, live client files in tests.

- ⊗ Using entire customer or employee datasets
- ⊗ Showing real names, emails, or IDs in demos
- ⊗ Testing with live client files or environments

5. Key controls: classify data, give prompt do/don't examples, strip files, enforce enterprise-approved tools.

- Classify data
- Provide do/don't examples
- Strip or redact files
- Use approved AI tools

What you Need to Remember

This is the most common everyday AI privacy risk.

People paste full customer lists, HR files, or financial data into AI tools to save time or get help.

Consumer AI tools may keep that data and use it to improve or train their models—unless you're on an enterprise plan with controls enabled.

The solution is simple but requires habit: share only the minimum data, anonymise where possible, and always know which tier of tool you are using.

1. Before you paste
Check if data is personal or sensitive.

2. If in doubt
Anonymise, sample, or use dummy data.

3. Right tool
Only upload sensitive data to approved enterprise AI with protections.

Consent, Notice, and Lawful Basis

- Every AI use of personal data must have a lawful basis (GDPR etc.)
- Common bases: consent, legitimate interests, contract, legal obligation
- Define lawful basis before deployment — don't retrofit
- Tell people when AI is processing their data
- Extra rules when AI decisions significantly affect people (GDPR Art. 22)

Choosing the right lawful basis

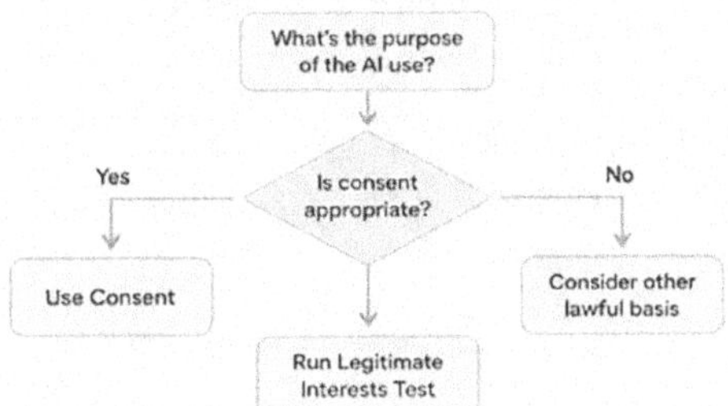

AI Project Intake — Lawful Basis

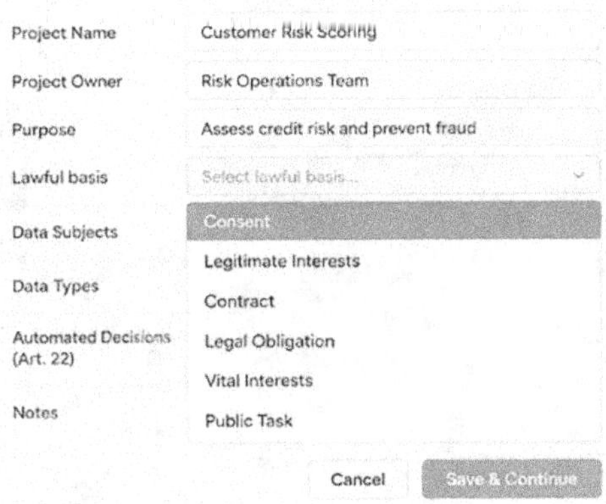

What you Need to Remember

Always define the legal basis for using personal data in AI systems before you build or deploy.

Legitimate interests can be a valid basis, but you must run and document a balancing test showing your interests don't override individual rights and freedoms.

Consent must be informed, specific, and freely given. It must be easy to understand and not a condition of a service, and it should never be buried in Terms & Conditions.

People have the right to know when AI is being used with their data and to receive clear, meaningful notice in plain language.

When AI decisions significantly affect people, they have the right to human review, to express their view, and to contest the decision (GDPR Art. 22).

1. Document your lawful basis
2. Run and record a legitimate interests test
3. Flag automated decisions needing human review

Section 3: Data, Security, and Privacy for AI Systems

3.3 Privacy and Personal Data in AI Operations

Employee Monitoring and Workplace AI

- AI tools track productivity, communications, meetings and behaviour patterns.
- Dashboards in tools like 365 analytics can surface individual and team data.
- Governance decides where productivity support ends and surveillance begins.
- Employees should know what's collected, how it's used, and how to correct errors.
- Controls: limit scope of monitoring, aggregate where possible, restrict access.
- Respect works councils, unions and local employment law requirements.

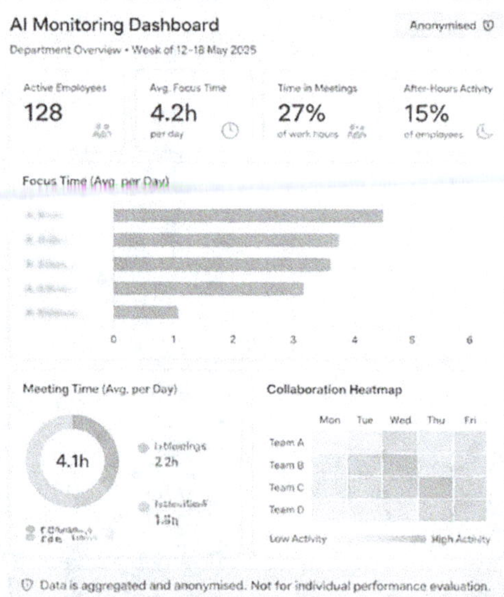

What you Need to Remember

This is a highly sensitive area of AI governance arriving through workplace analytics.

These tools can reveal hours in meetings, after-hours work patterns and networks of collaboration, which can easily be misused.

Legal rules vary by country (strong works council rules in some EU states, data protection duties in the UK, more permissive but mixed rules in the US).

Every organisation needs a documented policy: what is monitored, who sees it, level of detail, and allowed uses.

Employees should never have to guess whether keystrokes or messages are being logged.

- Design monitoring with purpose, not curiosity
- Default to aggregated, low-risk views for managers
- Explain monitoring clearly in onboarding and policy refreshes

Privacy Impact Assessments for AI

- DPIA is mandatory under GDPR for high-risk processing involving personal data.
- Most AI projects qualify: large-scale data, profiling, automated decisions, or sensitive information.
- Do it before deployment to catch risks early, not after a breach.
- Cover processing description, necessity, proportionality, risks, and mitigations.
- Add AI-specific checks: model behaviour risks, vendor data retention, and impact of outputs.
- Treat the DPIA as a living document and update when the system changes.

AI DPIA – Risk Summary — Edit Assessment

Overview | Processing | Risks | Mitigations | Approvals

Risk item	Likelihood	Impact	Status
Unfair bias in model outputs	Medium	High	Mitigating
Incorrect decisions affecting individuals	High	High	Mitigating
Excessive personal data collection	Medium	Medium	Planned
Vender data retention risk	Medium	High	Mitigating
Lack of transparency to data subjects	Low	Medium	Planned
Model drift over time	Medium	Medium	Planned

Overall risk level: Medium — Last updated: May 20, 2025

What you Need to Remember

DPIA is more than a checkbox; it tests whether an AI deployment is justified and what could go wrong for people.

Under GDPR, it's required where processing is likely high risk, which includes most AI using personal data.

It should ask: Is this necessary, are we minimising data, what happens if outputs are wrong, and what if the vendor changes retention?

Extend the DPIA template for AI vendor handling, harmful outputs, and end-of-life for the system.

Revisit the DPIA whenever the AI system or its use case changes significantly.

Before launch: Have we identified who could be harmed by this AI?

During use: Are we monitoring errors, complaints, and bias signals?

When things change: Do we re-run the DPIA after major model or vendor updates?

Data Lineage and Source Traceability

- Track where model inputs originate: databases, documents, APIs, prompts.
- Traceability lets you verify inputs are accurate, authorised, and current.
- RAG pipelines create complex chains that must stay auditable.
- Source metadata – author, date, system – should travel with the data.
- Broken lineage means decisions on stale, fabricated, or manipulated content.
- Governance teams should require documented lineage for AI approvals.

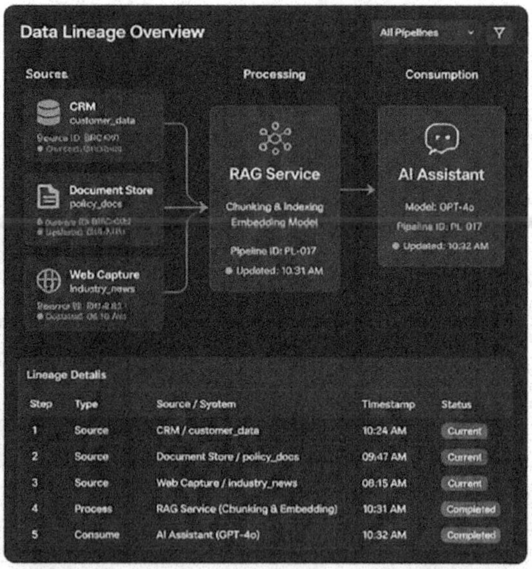

What you Need to Remember

Data lineage is the documented history of how data moves from its original source through each step of processing to the model output.

Without traceability, you cannot verify whether inputs were current, accurate, authorised, or tampered with.

RAG pipelines combine multiple sources — databases, documents, APIs, and the web — into a single answer, making lineage more complex but essential.

Source metadata such as author, date, system, and version must travel with the data so context is never lost.

Broken lineage creates real downstream risk — decisions can be based on stale, fabricated, or manipulated content. That's why governance frameworks now require documented lineage for AI approvals and audits.

Questions to Ask

- Can we show where this answer's data came from?
- Who owns and maintains the source?
- When was it last validated?
- What breaks if this lineage is wrong?

Output Verification and Citation Discipline

- AI can sound confident while being wrong — hallucinations are fluent but false answers.
- **Hallucinations are structured:** fake stats, cases, or specs that look legitimate.
- **Citation discipline = always ask:** 'Where did this come from?'
- **Models can invent sources** — titles, authors, URLs.
- **Match verification effort to risk:** light check for drafts, deep check for decisions.
- **Treat AI output as a draft only** — never final without human review.

AI Assistant

The company's remote work policy allows employees to work up to 2 days per week from home. This is outlined in the Remote Work Policy (v2.1, June 2024).

Sources

- Remote Work Policy (v2.1, June 2024)
- HR Guidelines – Flexible Working (2023)
- Employee Handbook (Section 4.2)

Source links (to be checked)

What you Need to Remember

AI will present wrong and right answers **in the same confident tone.**

Hallucinations can look like real data or citations.

Always demand and then verify sources.

Scale verification effort with the impact of the decision.

Organisation rule: **AI output is a starting point, not an authorised answer.**

- **High-risk use?** Require second human review.
- Spot-check citations before sharing outside the team.
- Make 'verify before you rely' a team habit.

Deepfakes, Synthetic Media, and Impersonation

- Synthetic audio, video, and images are now cheap, fast, and highly realistic.
- Deepfakes can convincingly impersonate executives, employees, and public figures.
- Risks: fraudulent approvals, fake briefings, manipulated 'evidence'.
- Attacks blend synthetic media with personal details scraped from public sources.
- Train staff to spot warning signs and verify requests via separate channels.
- Set clear rules for when synthetic media can be created and used internally.

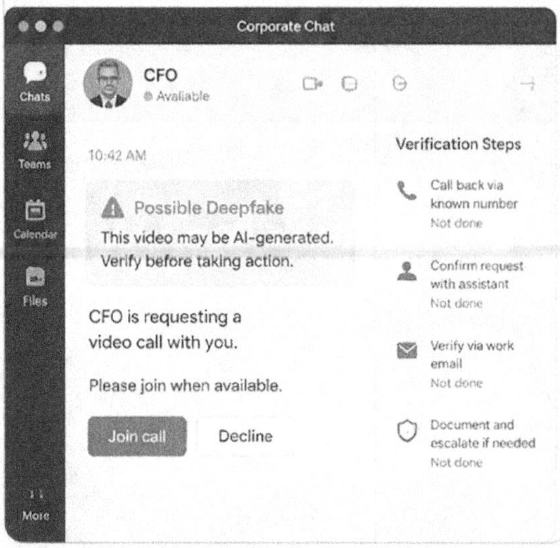

What you Need to Remember

Synthetic media is now a mainstream fraud and reputation risk.

Anyone can generate convincing voice or video of a familiar person.

Finance and approvals are prime targets – treat high-value requests as 'untrusted' until checked.

Combine technical controls with human processes: always confirm unusual requests through a known, separate channel.

Document when synthetic media is allowed so there's a visible line between sanctioned use and abuse.

- Use out-of-band checks for high-risk requests
- Escalate suspected deepfakes to security
- Review and update synthetic media policy annually

Watermarking, Provenance Signals, and Limits

AI watermarking
embeds signals in generated text, images, and audio to flag synthetic origin.

C2PA
an open standard for cryptographically signed provenance metadata on media files.

Watermarks can be stripped
or degraded – they're an aid, not a seal.

Text watermarks are fragile;
small edits, reformatting, or translation can erase them.

Provenance tools are improving
but don't fully solve authenticity.

Governance should use provenance
as one layer in a defence-in-depth strategy.

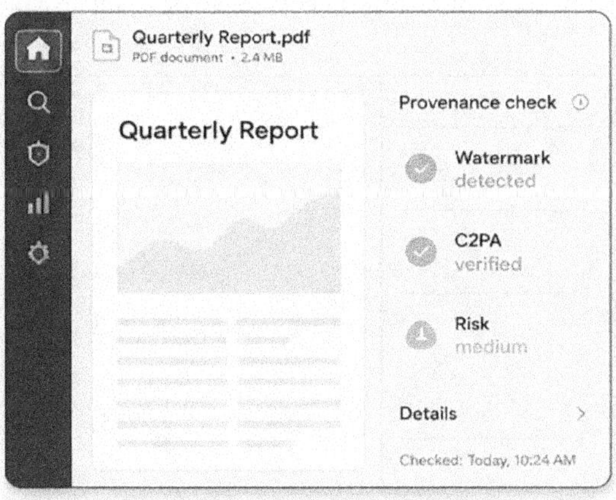

What you Need to Remember

Watermarking and C2PA labels help identify AI-generated content by embedding signals or metadata that indicate how, when, and with what tools content was created.

These signals can include statistical patterns in text, cryptographic metadata signatures in images and video, or inaudible markers in audio.

These controls are useful—but not foolproof. Watermarks can be removed or degraded, metadata can be stripped, and content can be re-edited or re-encoded to bypass detection.

Governance teams must combine provenance signals with clear policy, human review, and a culture of accountability—treating provenance as one layer in a broader, defence-in-depth approach.

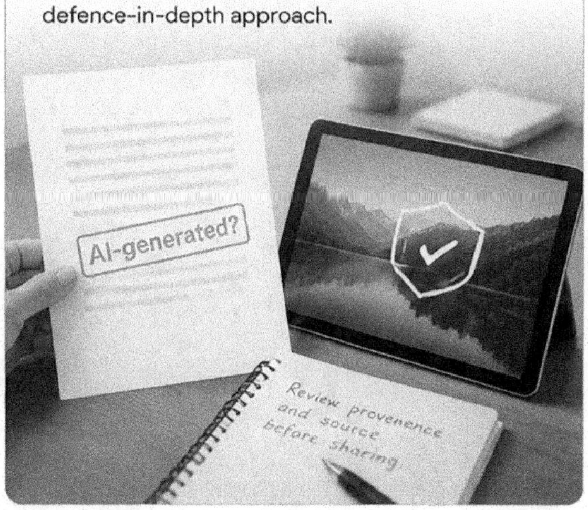

Where provenance helps most

- High-impact public communications
- Sensitive images and video
- Regulated reports and disclosures
- External vendor content

SECTION 4

Prompting, Agents, and Human Oversight

In this section, we look at how people interact with AI day to day: prompting well, using agents, and keeping meaningful human oversight. Prompting is a governance concern because a prompt's quality determines the reliability and safety of the output.

Five components make a strong prompt (role, context, task, format and constraints), structured patterns like Ask-Verify-Revise reduce risk, grounding is the most effective way to cut hallucination, and prompt libraries turn ad-hoc prompting into a governed workflow. We then explore agents: what makes a system agentic, when to use one rather than chat, the human-in-the-loop versus human-on-the-loop decision, and safe boundaries enforced in configuration.

We look at agent mode inside productivity tools, where AI drafts in Word, calculates in Excel and builds decks in PowerPoint, with tiered escalation ensuring high-stakes documents get an accountable reviewer.

Finally, we cover AI in automated workflows: APIs and function calling as governance boundaries, connectors and MCP expanding both capability and attack surface, comprehensive logging for accountability, and human review at scale matched to risk level, with review quality measured to guard against rubber-stamping.

Section 4: Prompting, Agents, and Human Oversight

4.1 Prompting as a Governance Issue

Prompt Design Fundamentals

Role – define the professional persona
Specify who the AI should act as, including expertise and perspective.

Task – state the action
Clearly describe the action or deliverable the AI should produce.

Context – give background not guesses
Provide relevant background, data, and objectives the AI should consider.

Constraints – set guardrails for safety and scope
Define boundaries, limits, and rules the AI must follow.

Output Format – say how results should be structured
Specify the structure, style, or format you need in the response.

AI Assistant

Use this template to create clear, governable prompts

Role	You are a compliance analyst with expertise in data privacy and AI governance.
Task	Review the scenario and identify key privacy risks and recommended controls.
Context	Our company uses an AI tool to summarise customer support tickets. Data includes names, email addresses, and issue details. Goal: assess privacy risks and ensure regulatory alignment.
Constraints	• Do not provide legal advice. • Focus on privacy and data protection only. • Keep the response under 300 words. • Reference applicable principles (e.g., GDPR).
Output Format	Provide a table with columns: Risk | Impact | Likelihood | Recommended Control Then add 3 key takeaways in bullet points.

+ Generate Response

In a governance context, a prompt is an instruction set that guides AI tools to produce accurate, relevant, and responsible outputs.

The quality of your Role, Task, Context, Constraints, and Output Format directly determines the reliability, safety, and auditability of the results.

Well-designed prompts reduce risk, improve consistency, and make AI outputs easier to review, verify, and act upon.

What you Need to Remember

- Define a clear role so the AI understands the expertise, perspective, and tone to use.
- Use strong action verbs in the task to make the objective specific and measurable.
- Provide enough context for the AI to reason well, including relevant background, data, and goals.
- Add constraints to set boundaries such as length, scope, sources to use, and what not to do (e.g., "don't give legal advice"). This improves safety and compliance.
- Specify the output format to get structured, consistent results that are easier to review, compare, and act on.

- Use all five components for important prompts.
- Test prompts with safe examples first.
- Review outputs for accuracy, bias, and compliance.
- Document approved prompt templates for reuse.

Prompt Patterns for Safer Work

Prompt patterns = repeatable structures that cut errors and support review.

Ask–Verify–Revise: prompt, inspect the answer, then refine.

Chain-of-Checks: ask for step-by-step reasoning before a conclusion.

Bounded instructions: tell the model to "only use the document / data provided".

Self-critique: ask the model to list weaknesses or gaps in its own answer.

Separate tasks: break big jobs into clear, sequential prompts.

Result: outputs are more predictable, reviewable and defensible.

AI Assistant

You 10:15 AM
Ask–Verify–Revise example
Summarize the key compliance requirements from the employee data policy PDF above.

Assistant 10:16 AM
Here is a summary of the key compliance requirements from the document:
- Purpose limitation and data minimisation
- Access controls and role-based permissions
- Data retention and secure disposal
- Incident reporting within 72 hours
- Employee rights and data access requests

Let me know if you'd like more detail on any of these.

You 10:18 AM
Now refine this based only on the policy PDF above.

Message AI Assistant...

AI responses can be inaccurate. Verify important information.

What you Need to Remember

Use prompt patterns as guardrails. Start with Ask–Verify–Revise so you never rely on the first answer. Combine Chain-of-Checks with Bounded Instructions to keep reasoning transparent and tied to approved sources.

Add self-critique prompts to surface risks or missing context. For complex work, split the job into smaller, auditable steps. Together, these patterns turn prompting into a repeatable, governable practice that supports AI ethics and oversight.

- Use patterns for high-risk or sensitive tasks.
- Keep prompts and outputs for audit trails.
- Agree shared patterns across your team.

Section 4: Prompting, Agents, and Human Oversight

4.1 Prompting as a Governance Issue

Reducing Hallucination Through Prompting

- **Define hallucination plainly:** model outputs plausible but wrong or invented content.
- Hallucinations increase when context is thin and tasks are very open-ended.
- Ground responses in provided documents, data or cited sources.
- Prompt for citations or source references.
- Use structured formats (tables, numbered steps, labelled sections) to separate fact from inference.
- Instruct the model to flag uncertainty instead of guessing.
- Reducing hallucinations is a compliance responsibility, not just best practice.

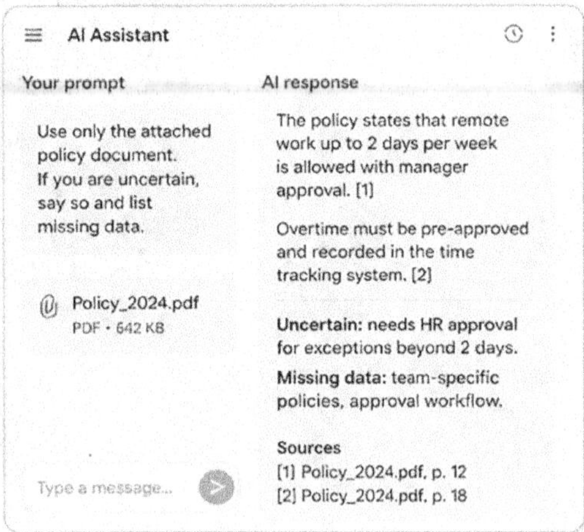

What you Need to Remember

Hallucination is a key enterprise AI risk because confident errors are harder to spot than clearly flagged gaps.

Grounding in real documents and data is the most powerful way to reduce it.

Asking for citations and uncertainty flags pushes the model toward transparency.

Structured outputs make review easier and stop errors from hiding in long prose.

In compliance and governance work, a response that openly shows its limits is safer than one that pretends to know.

Ground with sources | Use structure | Flag uncertainty

4.1 Prompting as a Governance Issue

Prompt Libraries and Controlled Templates

Ad hoc prompts = inconsistent quality and risk.

Library of tested prompts for common workflows (summaries, client emails, risk notes, data extraction).

Templates bake in tone, structure, legal and privacy rules.

Patterns reduce training load: staff adapt instead of inventing prompts.

Manage template versions like policy changes.

Restrict who can edit high-risk templates.

Library acts as evidence of standardised, reviewed AI use.

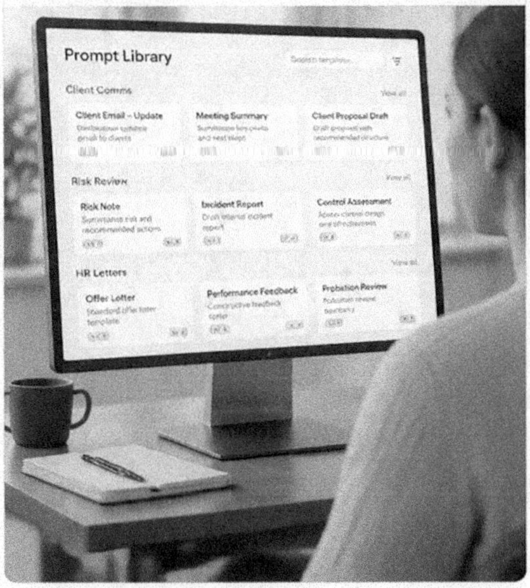

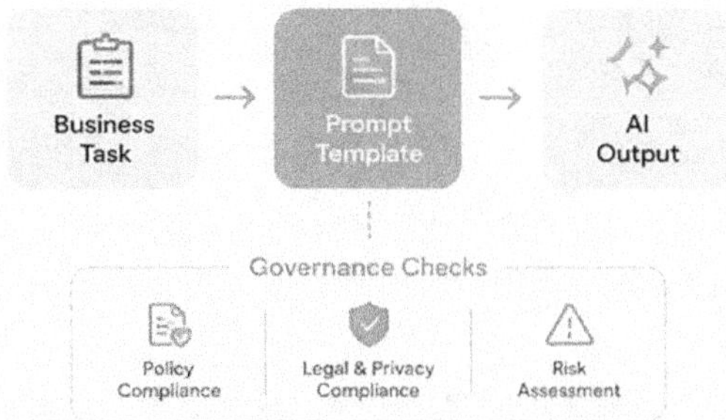

Prompt libraries turn proven, compliant ways of working into reusable templates for everyday tasks.

They standardise inputs, encode guardrails, and ensure outputs align with policy, tone, and regulatory obligations.

This reduces variation, improves quality, and lowers training needs—staff adapt templates instead of writing prompts from scratch.

Version control and access control provide oversight, so you can see who changed what, when, and why.

Together, these controls make prompt libraries a foundational part of AI governance.

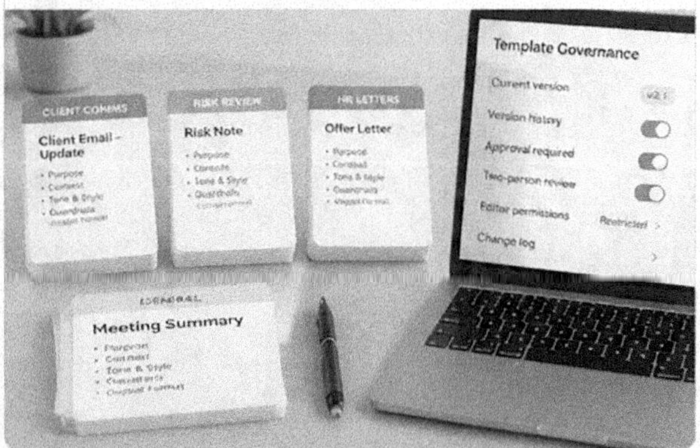

What you Need to Remember

If everyone prompts differently, you don't have a governed workflow. Prompt libraries are curated, approved templates that make the safe, compliant way the easiest.

Version and access controls show who changed what and when, creating accountablility and traceability.

A maintained library is evidence that your organisation uses AI responsibly and consistently.

When to update a prompt template: New policy or regulation | New risk identified or incident | Feedback shows better pattern

4.2 Working with AI Agents

What Makes an AI System Agentic

1. **Agents pursue goals**, not just single prompts.
2. **Goal pursuit:** work toward an outcome, like 'research and draft a briefing.'
3. **Tool use:** search, read files, call APIs, run code, and update systems.
4. **Memory:** retain context across steps, sessions, and data sources.
5. **Multistep action:** one request can trigger a chain of decisions and tasks.

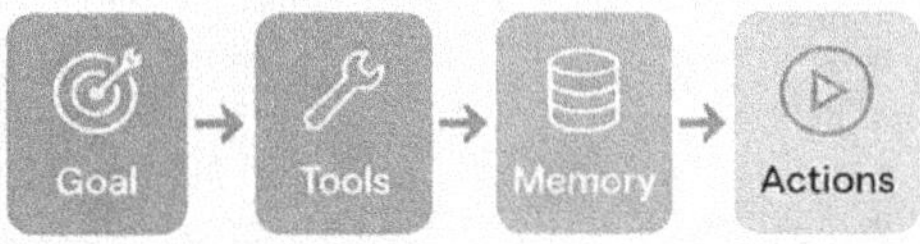

These four properties define agentic behavior.

Traditional chatbots respond to prompts and stop. Agentic AI systems go further—they pursue goals by planning, taking action, and learning as they go.

When given a goal, an agent figures out what needs to be done, chooses the right tools, gathers information, updates records, and checks results. If something changes, it adapts and keeps going.

This power creates value—but also risk. Agents can access data, change systems, and affect people. That's why governance matters. Clear goals, guardrails, monitoring, and human oversight ensure agents act safely, fairly, and in line with our values and policies.

What you Need to Remember

- Agents are designed to achieve goals, not just answer questions.
- They gain leverage from tools that let them read, write, and act in other systems.
- Memory lets them learn from previous steps and refine what they do next.
- Multistep action means one instruction can launch a whole workflow.
- Because agents can act, they demand stronger oversight and governance.

Define safe goals and boundaries for agents.

Log and review what agents do and which tools they use.

Set escalation rules: when must a human approve the next step?

4.2 Working with AI Agents

When to Use Agents Instead of Chat

1. Chat for single-turn drafting, Q&A, explanations.
2. Agents for repetitive, multi-step, or system-integrated tasks.
3. Research workflows across many sources.
4. Monitoring data and triggering actions.
5. Orchestrating sub-tasks across tools.
6. Rule of thumb: if multiple tools and steps are needed, an agent likely fits.

Chat	Agent
Single turn conversation	Multi-step workflows
One request at a time	Handles repetitive tasks
Uses provided context	Works across many systems
Quick responses	Runs over time, autonomously
Lower governance overhead	Higher governance requirements

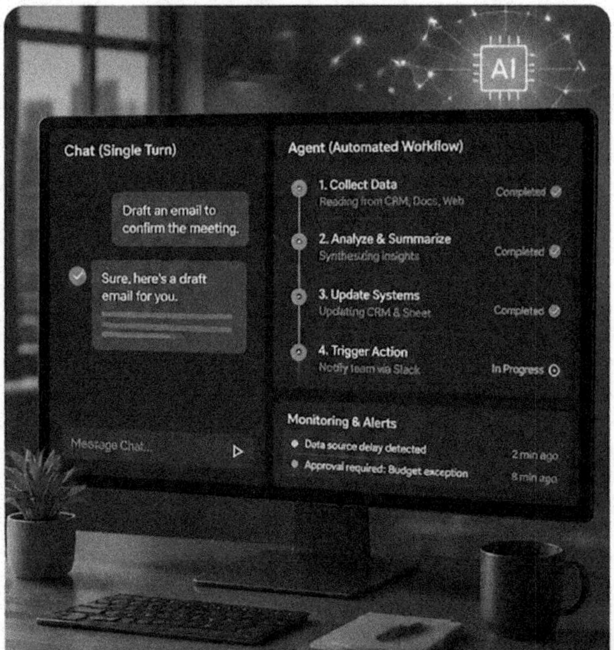

What you Need to Remember

- Choosing between chat and agents is a governance decision. The wrong choice can add risk, cost, and unnecessary complexity.
- Use chat for straightforward tasks like emails, summaries, and explanations.
- Use agents for multi-step, repetitive, or external-system workflows.
- Research, monitoring, and orchestration are classic agent use cases.
- Simple rule of thumb: if you'd open several tools and take multiple steps manually, consider an agent—but be prepared for higher governance stakes.

When an Agent is Worth It

- Cross-system research loop
- Always-on monitoring
- Complex approvals and workflows
- Data updates across multiple tools

Section 4: Prompting, Agents, and Human Oversight

4.2 Working with AI Agents

Human-in-the-Loop vs Human-on-the-Loop

Human-in-the-loop

- Agent pauses for approval at key steps
- Best for high-stakes, irreversible, or regulated actions
- Used for sending payments, publishing external content, legal sign-off.

Human-on-the-loop

- Agent runs autonomously, human monitors
- Best for low-risk, reversible or high-volume tasks
- Used for drafting, formatting, internal summaries.

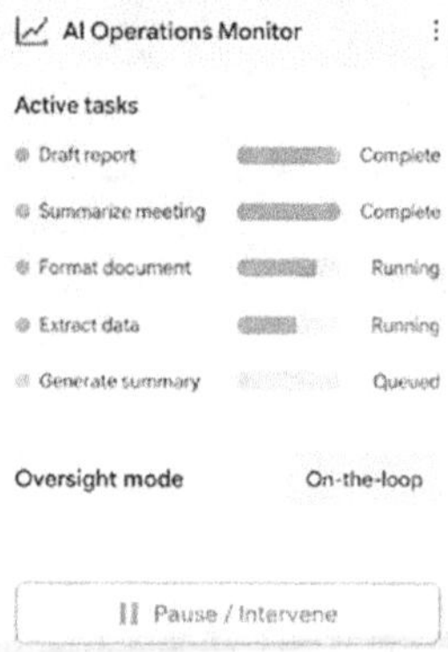

Choosing the supervision pattern

- High impact / hard to undo? → In-the-loop
- Low impact / reversible? → On-the-loop

What you Need to Remember

Oversight level is a key AI design decision.

In-the-loop = mandatory checkpoints before certain actions.

On-the-loop = continuous monitoring without step-by-step approval.

Neither pattern is always better; match oversight to risk, reversibility, and volume.

Document which pattern applies to each workflow and review as systems mature.

Many tools support configurable checkpoints mixing both approaches.

Useful checks when designing oversight

- Risk & reversibility
- Regulation & policy
- Volume & speed needs
- Who is accountable?
- Where to place checkpoints?

Safe Agent Boundaries

Scope limits
Define what the agent can access and do.

Least-privilege access
Give only the minimum permissions needed.

Approval gates
Require human approval for sensitive actions.

Kill switch / pause
Stop or pause the agent immediately if needed.

Logging & audit trail
Log actions, decisions, and changes for traceability.

Boundary failures risk
Understand risks if the agent operates outside its limits.

Agent Access Map (Safe Boundaries)

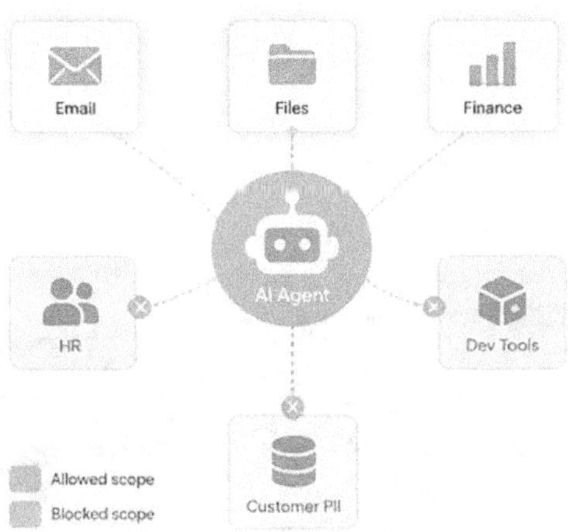

Controls and boundaries are what make AI agents reliable and safe to use.

By defining clear limits, access rules, and approval steps, you reduce risk, protect sensitive data, and keep agents aligned with your business goals.

These controls are not "set and forget". Review boundaries regularly as your systems, teams, and work evolve.

What you Need to Remember

When to Review Agent Boundaries

- New data sources added
- Role or team changes
- Regulation or policy updates
- Incident or near-miss
- Expansion to new workflows

Agent Mode in Workplace Productivity Tools

1. From Chat to Action
Agent mode lets AI directly edit Word, Excel and PowerPoint files, not just answer questions.

2. Embedded in Microsoft 365
Copilot is now inside core tools, making AI assistance part of everyday work.

3. Governance Shift
Once AI can act on live documents, risk moves from wrong answers to wrong changes.

4. Business Artifacts at Stake
Edits can affect contracts, models and decks that may be shared or published.

5. Tool-by-Tool Oversight
Each app needs clear rules for what AI may change and when humans must step in.

What you Need to Remember

AI agents are now built into the tools where work happens—Word, Excel and PowerPoint—so they can create, summarise and edit your files directly.

When AI can modify real documents and data, the consequences go beyond incorrect answers—they can create inaccurate reports, flawed models or misleading presentations that travel far.

Your team must decide when human review is mandatory, what changes AI is allowed to make, and how every action is tracked before anything leaves your organisation.

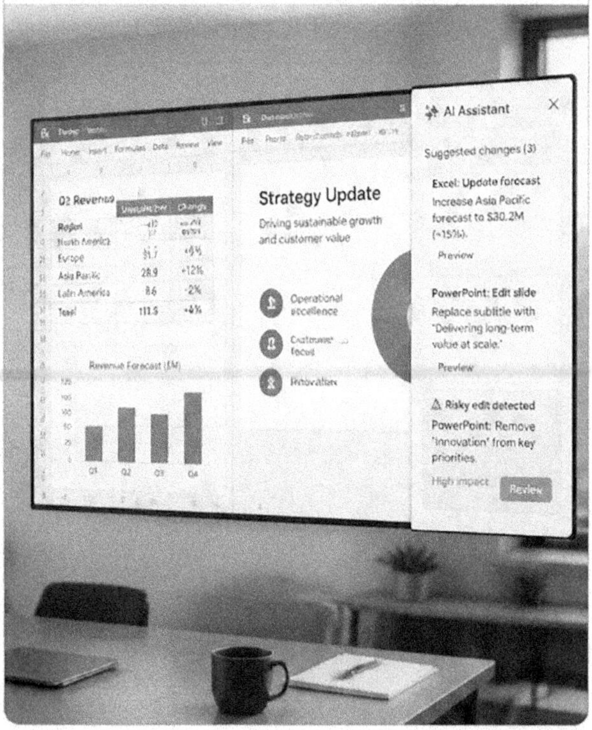

Require human sign-off for:

1) Client-facing documents

2) Regulatory or legal content

3) Financial models and forecasts

4) Public announcements or board materials

Section 4: Prompting, Agents, and Human Oversight

4.3 Agent Mode in Workplace Productivity Tools

Agent Mode in Word — Drafting, Rewriting, and Document Transformation with Oversight

Draft, rewrite, and transform.
Copilot can draft from scratch, rewrite sections, adjust tone, and restructure documents.

Summarise and extract key insights.
It can summarise long files, extract key points, and suggest follow-up actions.

AI drafts are a starting point.
Treat every AI draft as a starting point, not a final version.

Higher risk for high-stakes docs.
Risk is highest for contracts, policies, reports, and client-facing documents.

Use Track Changes and history.
Use Track Changes and version history as core audit and oversight tools.

Policy defines mandatory review.
Your policy should define which document types require mandatory human review.

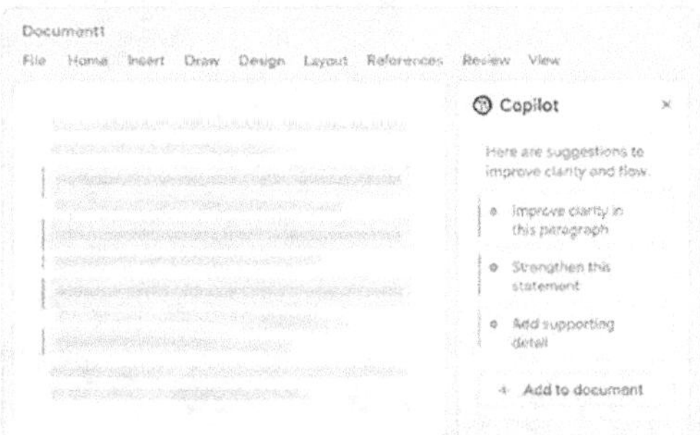

AI-assisted draft

What you Need to Remember

In Microsoft Word, Copilot appears in "agent mode" — visible in the side pane and ready to act on your prompt. From a short instruction, it can generate full drafts, rewrite sections, and transform documents in seconds.

Risk is not the same for every document. Internal notes may be low risk; contracts, policies, reports, or client-facing materials carry much higher stakes. Always consider the audience and impact.

AI-generated text is a starting point, not sign-off. You are accountable for accuracy, tone, compliance, and confidentiality. Never publish or share without thorough human review.

Use Track Changes and version history to review every edit, compare drafts, and explain decisions. Require named reviewers and approvals as defined in your acceptable use policy.

When to slow down and double-check AI in Word

- Client proposals
- Contracts & terms
- Policies & HR comms
- Regulatory or audit reports
- Anything signed or externally shared

Agent Mode in Excel — Analysis, Spreadsheet Changes, and Formula Risk Management

- Copilot can build formulas, new columns, pivots, and reshape tables in seconds.
- It can explain trends, flag outliers, and summarise numbers in plain language.
- AI-written formulas look normal — errors may hide in plain sight.
- Financial models, pricing tools, and standard reports are highest-risk for silent errors.
- Always test AI formulas with known sample values before rollout.
- Lock key cells, ranges, and sheets so AI can't rewrite critical logic.

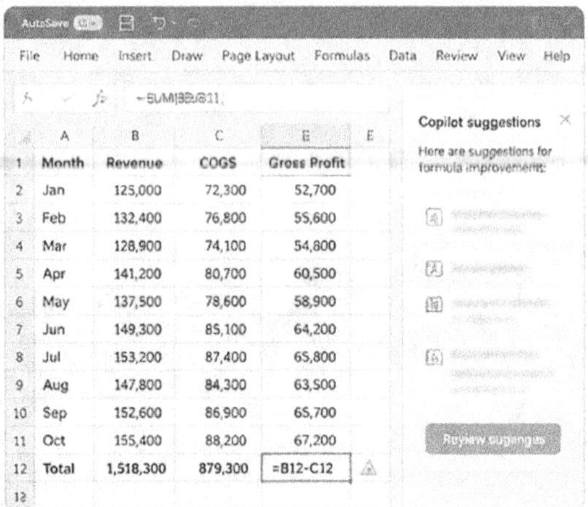

What you Need to Remember

Excel is where AI mistakes turn into real financial impact.

Copilot can quietly change formulas, structures, and calculated columns, and a single wrong formula can flow through budgets and reports without being noticed.

Treat AI edits like code changes: test them against trusted numbers, add a review step for high-stakes workbooks, and use protections to fence off the parts of models that drive decisions or regulators care about.

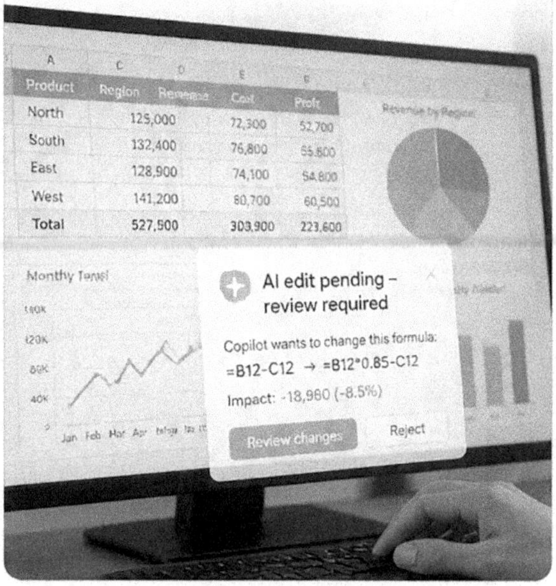

1. Classify the spreadsheet: low, medium, or high impact.
2. Test AI-generated formulas with sample data.
3. Require human sign-off for high-impact or regulated files.

4.3 Agent Mode in Workplace Productivity Tools

Agent Mode in PowerPoint — Automated Presentation Building and Review Responsibilities

- **Generate full decks from a prompt** or Word file
- **Auto-add slides, layouts, notes,** and suggested images
- **Fast output tempts people to share** before review
- **Main risks: brand compliance,** factual accuracy, confidentiality
- **Slides may contain plausible but** wrong or outdated claims
- **High-stakes audiences always** need human accuracy review

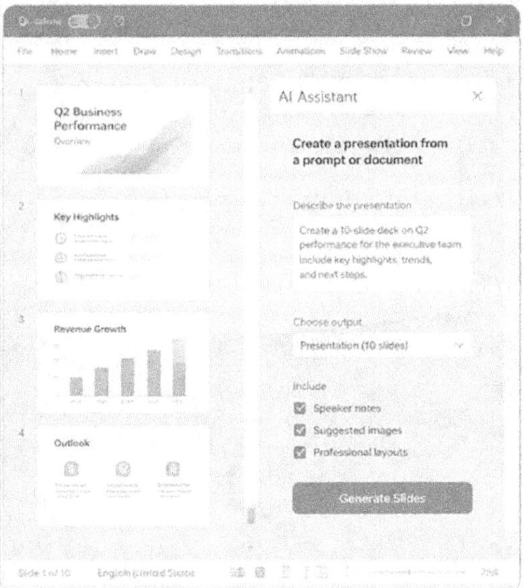

What you Need to Remember

Agent Mode in PowerPoint is incredibly fast and convenient. That speed is its biggest seduction — and the main driver of risk.

AI can produce professional-looking decks with confident charts, statistics, and branding — even when the content is incorrect, outdated, or not aligned to brand and compliance standards.

Confidential internal information can be unintentionally included in external presentations, creating legal, regulatory, and reputational risk.

The higher the consequence of the audience (clients, boards, regulators), the more thorough and documented the human review must be.

When extra review is essential

Client-facing presentations	Board or regulator briefings	Slides with sensitive internal data	External marketing or sales decks	Any slide containing statistics or data

Escalation Points in Office Workflows — When Humans Must Review Before Publication or Sharing

Legal or regulatory content
Escalate all content that could create legal, compliance, or policy obligations.

Client-facing materials
Human review required for proposals, reports, contracts, and external comms.

Financial data or calculations
Escalate any AI-generated numbers, forecasts, or financial analysis.

HR or people decisions
Escalate content affecting hiring, performance, pay, discipline, or employee data.

Substantial AI rewrite
If AI makes material changes to your original input, escalate for review.

Named reviewer role
A specific person with the right expertise must approve before publication or sharing.

Low Risk
AI draft + Self-check
↓
Medium Risk
AI draft + Peer Review
↓
High Risk
AI draft + Expert Review + Final Approval

What you Need to Remember

Place human oversight where it adds real value—focus on areas with impact, risk, or ethical sensitivity.

Define clear escalation triggers so the right content reaches the right reviewers consistently.

Avoid "rubber-stamp" review—challenge assumptions, verify facts, and consider bias and edge cases.

Log AI involvement and reviewer actions to maintain transparency and support accountability.

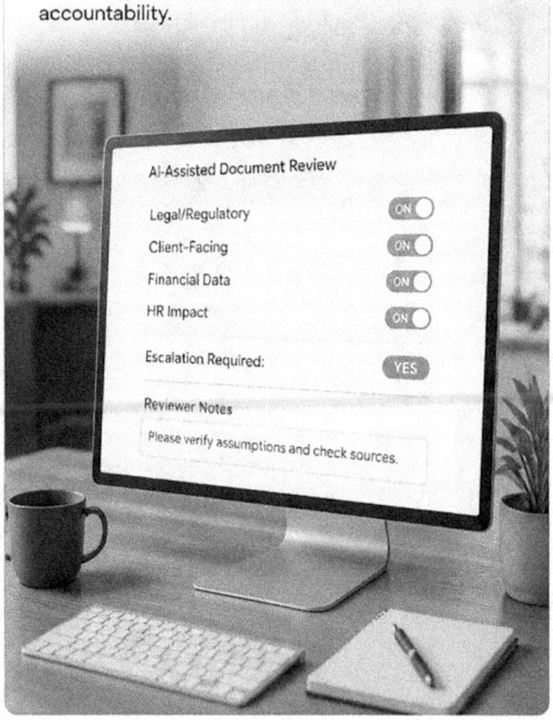

Document risk level first | Assign a named reviewer | Log AI involvement

API-Based AI Workflows

Governance boundary
The line between casual consumer prompting (person or team) and governed applications (organizational use with controls).

Embedded in tools & pipelines
The API lets AI power internal tools, automation, and products.

Fewer safety rails
API use bypasses consumer UI guardrails, so governance must replace them.

Key questions
Who can call the API, what data can they send, and what controls apply?

Approval needed
Organizational sign-off before production use.

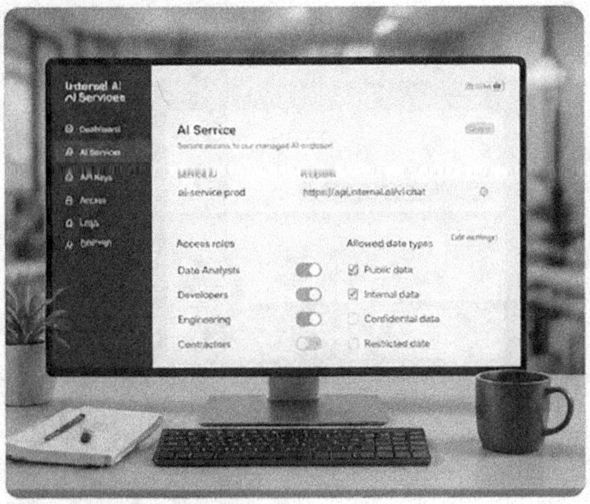

What you Need to Remember

Moving from chat to API is a governance boundary.

API calls embed AI into workflows, automations, and products—and expose raw model behaviour.

The responsibility for safety, data handling, and accountability shifts from the provider's consumer UI to your organization.

Before enabling API access, answer three critical questions:

1) Who is authorized? 2) What data is allowed? 3) What controls apply?

Put the right controls in place, then approve, monitor, and iterate.

1. Define use case & data
Clarify the goal, data sources, and required AI capabilities. →

2. Design controls & logging
Define access, data handling, guardrails, and audit logging. →

3. Approve & monitor API use
Obtain sign-off, enable access, and continuously monitor for safety and performance.

Function Calling and Tool Invocation

- Lets AI trigger real-world actions, not just generate text.
- Common tools: web search, databases, calculators, file ops, APIs.
- Every tool call is a real action — treat it with governance.
- Limit scope: define which tools can run and when.
- Add human approval before high-impact or irreversible actions.

What you Need to Remember

Function calling turns a language model into an actor. Each call can query live data, run calculations, write or update records, or trigger external systems.

Because these actions have real consequences, you control them through narrow tool permissions and human approval for anything hard to undo.

USEFUL PROMPTS FOR SAFER TOOL USE

- Ask model to explain why it needs a tool
- Require confirmation before critical actions
- Log every tool call
- Test tools in a sandbox first

Connectors, MCP, and External System Access

- **AI connectors link assistants** to external systems and data sources.
- **MCP is an emerging standard** that enables secure, consistent integration across platforms.
- **Every connector expands** the attack surface and potential data exposure.
- **Design permissions with** least privilege and purpose-based access.
- **Govern connectors continuously** through reviews, monitoring, and documented approvals.

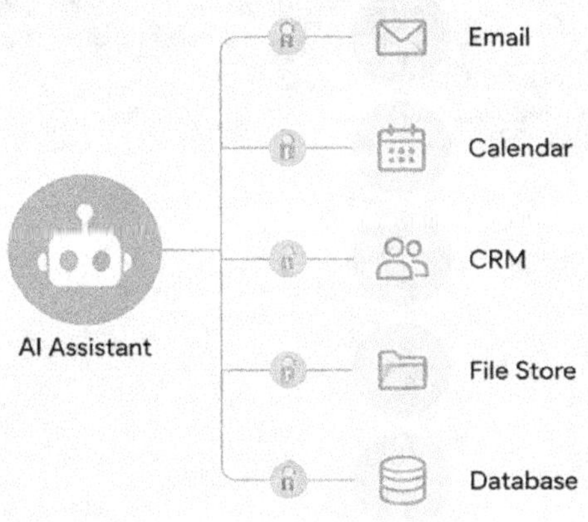

What you Need to Remember

Connectors allow AI assistants to reach beyond their native environment to retrieve, update, and act on external data and systems.

The Model Context Protocol (MCP) is an emerging standard that aims to make these integrations more secure, consistent, and interoperable.

Every connection introduces risk. Apply least privilege, scope access to specific purposes, and limit data exposure to only what's necessary.

Strong governance—approval workflows, inventory, reviews, and monitoring—helps ensure connectors remain secure, necessary, and aligned with business and compliance requirements.

- New connector requested
- High-risk data involved
- Role changes
- Incident or near-miss

Logging, Observability, and Replay

- Log every automated AI action
- Capture inputs, tool calls, outputs, timestamps
- Use observability dashboards to flag anomalies and policy breaches
- Enable exact workflow replay for incident investigation
- Align log retention with legal, regulatory, and incident-response requirements

Comprehensive logging is the foundation of trust and accountability in AI systems.

By capturing every automated action—inputs, tool calls, outputs, and timestamps—you create a complete audit trail of what happened and why.

Observability dashboards help you detect anomalies and policy breaches early, so issues can be addressed before they escalate.

When incidents occur, exact workflow replay lets you reconstruct and understand events step by step.

Finally, retaining logs per legal, regulatory, and incident-response requirements ensures you're prepared for audits, investigations, and continuous improvement.

What you Need to Remember

Log every action, monitor for issues, replay workflows when needed, and retain logs according to policy. Together, these practices create transparency, enable faster incident response, and demonstrate accountability across your AI systems.

Workflow Run

Log every step

Monitor for anomalies

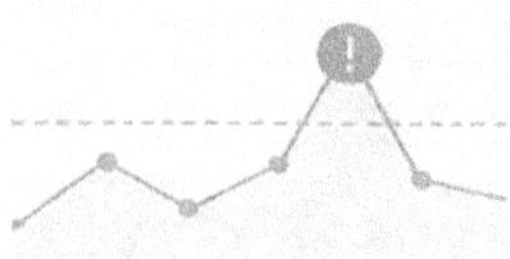

Set retention by policy

4.5 Review, Verification, and Approval Design

Review Checkpoints by Risk Level

- Oversight should match the real-world risk of the AI output.
- **Low-risk:** internal drafts, quick notes.
  - Light review: read, sense-check, move on.
- **Medium-risk:** client content, analysis.
  - Structured check against facts or checklist.
- **High-risk:** decisions, recommendations, regulated comms.
  - Formal sign-off by a named accountable person.
- Define tiers at the use-case level, not ad hoc.
- Tiered review avoids both rubber-stamping and review fatigue.

What you Need to Remember

Match depth of human review to the stakes of the AI output.

Light-touch checks for internal drafts and summaries.

Structured reviews for anything external or used for analysis.

Named sign-off for outputs linked to important decisions or regulated topics.

Pre-defined tiers make governance consistent, not performative.

AI Governance

Overview | Use-Cases | Reviews | Policies | Reports

Use-Case	Risk Level	Required Review	Owner	Status
Internal Drafts	Low	Spot check	Marketing	Active
Meeting Summaries	Low	Spot check	Corporate Ops	Active
Market Analysis	Medium	Checklist	Strategy	Active
Client Reports	Medium	Checklist	Consulting	Active
Decision Support	High	Formal sign-off	Operations	Active
Regulated Comms	High	Formal sign-off	Legal	Active

Set risk tiers for each use-case

Define review steps per tier

Name accountable reviewers for high-risk work

4.5 Review, Verification, and Approval Design

Output Validation Techniques

- Fact-check specific claims against trusted sources.
- Run policy checks for legal, compliance and brand fit.
- Use scenario tests by nudging inputs and watching how outputs change.
- Cross-reference against trusted human or validated material.
- Use structured review forms, not blank sign-off boxes.
- Always record what you checked and what you found.

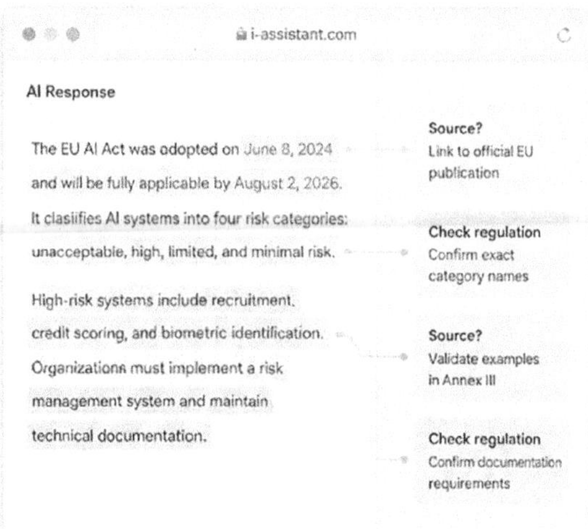

What you Need to Remember

Good review is active validation, not just reading.

Confirm facts and references with trusted sources.

Check against policies, regulations, and risk considerations.

Probe scenarios by changing inputs to see how outputs respond.

Compare outputs with trusted human expertise or validated material.

Use structured questions and checklists to guide your review.

Document what you checked and what you found—undocumented checks don't count.

Design review form	Define trusted sources	Escalate high-risk outputs	Track validation metrics

Exception Handling and Escalation

- AI can fail, hallucinate or give unsafe responses.
- Governance defines the playbook — not improvisation.
- Reviewers must know what counts as an exception and who to notify.
- Route issues differently for wrong answers vs. policy violations.
- Sometimes pause or withdraw tools while issues are investigated.
- Capture 'near-miss' incidents to reveal control gaps.

What you Need to Remember

Unexpected or problematic AI outputs are inevitable. Good governance means defining what an exception is and capturing it consistently.

Have a clear escalation path that separates operational errors from policy breaches so issues reach the right people fast.

Sometimes the right call is to pause or withdraw a tool while you investigate and reduce risk.

Near-misses are valuable signals. Capture them too—they help you strengthen controls and prevent future incidents.

- Log every incident
- Close the loop with users
- Feed learnings back into model and policy design

Measuring Review Quality

- **Spot rubber-stamping:** reviews that are fast, automatic, and never question the AI.
- **Don't rely on speed and volume metrics alone.**
- **Track signals of real scrutiny:** time spent, questions, edits, and escalations.
- **Run calibration tests** with deliberately flawed outputs.
- **Capture rich audit trails:** who reviewed, when, and what changed.
- **Monitor review quality trends over time,** not just completion rates.

Review Session Log

Last 7 days

Reviewer	Time Spent (min)	Questions	Edits	Escalations
Aisha Khan	18	4	3	1
Marcus Lee	22	6	5	2
Emma Patel	15	2	2	0
Daniel Ruiz	9	0	0	0
Priya Singh	24	7	6	3

Healthy · Monitor · Investigate

Good review quality is about challenge and calibration, not throughput. High-quality reviews involve thoughtful questions, careful edits, and timely escalations when something doesn't look right.

By tracking the right signals, running calibration tests, and analysing trends over time, you can ensure reviews catch issues before they become real-world harm. Quality oversight builds trust, reduces risk, and makes AI systems safer and more reliable.

What you Need to Remember

- **A fast review that never pushes back is a risk signal, not a success.**
- **Measure how often reviewers question, amend, or escalate.**
- **Use calibration tests with known issues to check if oversight is working.**
- **Analyse review data over time so silent failures don't creep in.**

Example review quality KPIs
% items with comments or edits
Escalations per 100 items
Avg. review time

When to investigate
Sudden drop in escalations
Low comment or edit rates
Very short review times

Who should see this data
Governance leads, risk, and team managers

SECTION 5

Governance of Generative AI Content and Decisions

In this section, we look at how organisations govern the content generative AI produces and the decisions it informs, where polished, confident output can mask serious risk. The challenge is not simply preventing obviously harmful content, but recognising that plausible, professional-looking material can be inaccurate, inappropriate or damaging and still pass unnoticed through normal workflows. We open with problematic content: harmful material produced even from innocent intent; misleading, off-brand or reputationally damaging outputs that go unchecked because they look polished; contested copyright and ownership questions, since models are trained on web-scraped material; and content moderation framed as quality and safety assurance rather than censorship. Controls need to reflect where content is going: an internal draft does not carry the same exposure as something sent to a client, regulator or the public, and someone must ultimately own the output before it leaves the organisation.

We then turn to bias, fairness and inclusion, focusing on concrete situations where real people are treated differently because of how a system was built or used. We examine the sources of bias, how fairness differs for generative and decision-support tools, bias testing and red teaming, including comparative prompting, which runs structurally identical prompts differing only in demographic details, and inclusive design with meaningful routes to explanation and appeal. The emphasis is on detecting unequal outcomes in practice rather than assuming that apparently neutral technology will necessarily produce neutral results.

The section then addresses explainability and decision quality: why explainability in LLM-based systems is genuinely hard; why confidence and uncertainty reporting matters when models can sound equally convincing when right or wrong; and the clear line between decision support, where AI informs a human judgement, and decision making, where the system itself determines an outcome. The latter carries much greater ethical and legal exposure, particularly in areas such as hiring, lending and clinical triage. Documentation for high-stakes use is therefore a governance requirement, allowing the organisation to show what the AI produced, what evidence was considered, what the human did with the output, and who ultimately made the final call.

The largest part of the section is incident management. We define AI incidents and near misses, with the latter acting as the canary in the coal mine, and set out what must be reported, to whom, and against which triggers, including individual harm, potential data breaches, safety-critical failures, and regulatory or press exposure. Investigation and root-cause analysis group AI failures into prompt, data, tool and model categories, helping organisations move beyond simply blaming the user or the technology. We also emphasise immediate evidence preservation, because logs, prompt histories and other records can expire quickly, making it much harder to reconstruct what happened after the event.

Together, these controls provide a practical framework for governing what AI says, how its outputs influence consequential decisions, and how organisations respond when something goes wrong.

Section 5: Governance of Generative AI Content and Decisions

5.1 Content Risk in Generative AI

Harmful, Misleading, and Manipulative Outputs

1) Harmful outputs

- May promote violence or self-harm.
- Can include discriminatory or hateful content.
- Might encourage illegal or dangerous activity.

2) Misleading outputs

- Can contain hallucinated facts.
- May include fake citations or sources.
- Provide plausible but incorrect answers with high confidence.

AI Assistant Today

Who wrote the book "The Signal and the Noise"?

The book *The Signal and the Noise* was written by **Nate Silver.**

Source: Silver, N. (2011). *The Signal and the Noise: Why So Many Predictions Fail—But Some Don't.* Crown Publishing.

This answer is incorrect. The book was written by Nate Silver.

3) Manipulative outputs

- Can use persuasive text that exploits cognitive biases.
- May unfairly influence choices or decisions.

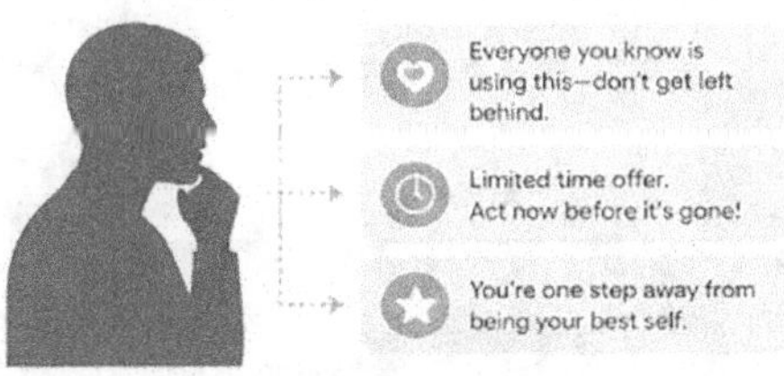

Risks apply across all media types

Text	Images	Audio	Video

The same harmful, misleading, and manipulative risks can appear in text, images, audio, and video.

What you Need to Remember

Problematic AI content isn't just a technical issue—it's a governance responsibility. It can cause real harm to people, damage trust, and create legal and reputational risk.

AI outputs can be harmful, misleading, or manipulative—even when prompts are harmless or well-intentioned. Understanding the difference helps you identify and manage the right risks.

Risks aren't limited to text. Images, audio, and video can also be false, biased, or used to manipulate—often with greater impact.

Governance is not a one-time check. It requires ongoing monitoring, clear policies, human oversight, and a culture of accountability to keep AI systems safe and trustworthy.

Check for:

Safety (violence/ self-harm)	Accuracy (facts & sources)	Fairness (bias & impact)	Influence (nudging & pressure)	Media Type (text, image, audio, video)	Ongoing Review (logs & escalation)

Section 5: Governance of Generative AI Content and Decisions

5.1 Content Risk in Generative AI

Brand, Reputational, and Communication Risk

- Unreviewed AI content can cause reputational damage or regulatory attention.
- Risky examples: inaccurate press releases, hallucinated data in client docs, off-tone social posts.
- Brand risk scales with speed and volume of AI output.
- Fluent AI text hides errors—people may not notice.
- Match governance to content type and audience; public and regulated outputs need stricter checks.
- Assign clear review and sign-off ownership before content is released.

AI Draft Checker

Channel	Risk Level	Reviewer Assiont	[illegible]
Press	High	Yes	Needs Changes
Client	Medium	Yes	Needs Changes
Social	Low	No	Approved

What you Need to Remember

AI outputs can look polished—but they can still be wrong, off-brand, or misleading.

Organisations feel the impact as brand damage, customer loss, or regulatory scrutiny—not just internal mistakes.

Speed and scale mean more content goes out faster than legacy review processes can keep up.

Apply tiered controls based on destination. Internal content needs lighter checks; client, regulatory, and public-facing content require stronger review and validation.

Always assign named accountability for the final sign-off. Every AI-assisted output needs a responsible human owner.

When to Slow Down
Sensitive audiences, high-visibility announcements.

Extra Checks
Stats, legal or regulatory references.

Who Owns It
Name a human approver for every AI-assisted output.

Section 5: Governance of Generative AI Content and Decisions

5.1 Content Risk in Generative AI

Copyright and Ownership Questions

Training data sources
AI models learn from large amounts of data. Datasets may include copyrighted works—sometimes without permission.

Legal status is contested
Courts are still deciding how copyright law applies to AI training, outputs, and ownership of AI-generated content.

Risk of infringement
Outputs that reproduce or closely resemble copyrighted material or code may infringe third-party rights.

Commercial use increases stakes
Using AI outputs commercially raises risk. Check tool terms, licence limits, and indemnity; don't assume ownership.

Attribution and disclosure matter
Provide clear attribution where required. Transparency builds trust and reduces reputational and legal risk.

Governance and documentation
Follow organisation policies, document sources and decisions, and keep records of reviews and approvals.

AI Training Pipeline – Copyright Checkpoints

Web Content → AI Training → Model Output → Human Review

- **Web Content**: Check source rights and licences
- **AI Training**: Ensure lawful use for training purposes
- **Model Output**: Check for similarity or reproduction
- **Human Review**: Approve, edit and document decisions

What you Need to Remember

The law is still evolving. Ownership of AI-generated content and the legality of training on copyrighted material remain uncertain and vary by jurisdiction.

Infringement risks exist. Outputs that reproduce recognisable text, images, music, or code may infringe rights and lead to takedowns, claims, or penalties.

Higher stakes for commercial use. Commercial deployment increases liability. Review tool terms, licence restrictions, and indemnity before relying on outputs.

Transparency and policy protect everyone. Attribute sources when required, disclose AI use, and follow clear governance policies with documented human oversight.

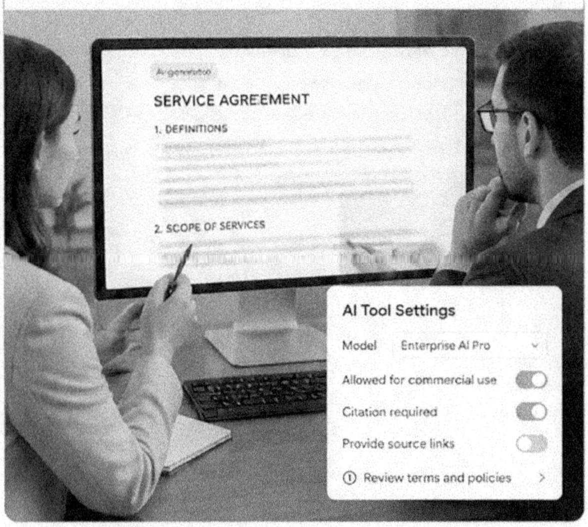

When to escalate to Legal
If outputs may infringe copyright, include third-party content, or will be used commercially.

Red flags in AI outputs
Verbatim text, long passages, watermarks, logos, or code that matches existing sources.

Safe uses of generative AI
Ideation, drafting, summarising public info, and non-sensitive internal content.

Where to find your organisation's AI policy
Check the intranet, policy hub, or contact your AI governance team.

Content Moderation Strategies

Use platform filters.
Enable built-in safety filters to block harmful, unsafe, or policy-violating content at the source.

Shape behaviour with prompts.
Apply system prompts and templates that set tone, scope, and boundaries for acceptable outputs.

Review what matters.
Route high-risk or high-impact outputs to human reviewers before they're shared or acted on.

Restrict how AI is used.
Limit access, capabilities, and data sources based on role, risk, and business need.

Calibrate continuously.
Monitor performance, learn from feedback, and update controls to address new risks.

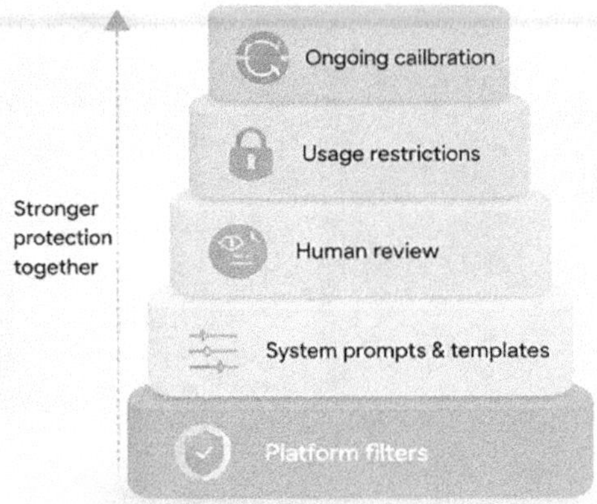

Effective content moderation for AI isn't one control—it's a layered system.

Start with platform safety filters to block harmful or policy-violating content. Use prompts and templates to guide model behaviour and keep outputs on track.

Route high-risk or high-impact outputs to human reviewers. Restrict access and capabilities based on role and risk.

Then, monitor outcomes, learn from feedback, and tune your controls over time.

This defence-in-depth approach reduces risk, builds trust, and supports responsible AI at scale.

What you Need to Remember

- Frame moderation as quality and safety assurance—not just compliance.
- Platform/vendor filters help, but your organisation owns the controls and accountability.
- Use system prompts and templates to set clear guardrails and constrain model behaviour.
- Require a named human approver for high-risk or high-impact outputs.
- Apply tiered access to AI capabilities and data based on role and risk.
- Controls are not "set and forget"—review and update them regularly.

Set guardrails | Define review points | Assign owners | Review and update controls

Sources of Bias in Modern AI Systems

Bias can enter at any stage of an AI system's lifecycle — design, data, prompts, and use.

Training data: models mirror patterns in historical data, including past inequalities.

Prompting: vague tasks like "find the best" can trigger hidden assumptions.

Retrieval: gaps or skews in knowledge bases are passed straight through to outputs.

User context: personalisation and history-based suggestions can reinforce existing views.

Seeing where bias starts is the first step to governing it.

Bias in AI systems is not just a technical issue — it's about real people and the risk of unequal treatment.

It can be introduced through training data that reflects historical inequities, through prompts that carry hidden assumptions, through retrieval sources that are incomplete or skewed, and through personalised user context that reinforces existing preferences and behaviours.

Understanding where bias originates allows teams to take targeted action, reduce harm, and build fairer, more trustworthy systems.

Strong AI governance means examining every stage of the workflow, setting clear standards, and continuously monitoring for unfair outcomes.

When we know where bias can enter, we can design better safeguards and create AI that serves everyone more equitably.

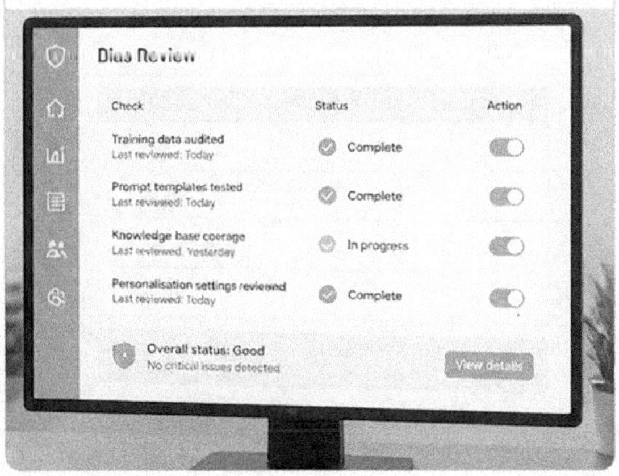

Audit data sources

Test high-impact prompts

Review knowledge bases

Monitor personalisation effects

Fairness in Generative and Decision-Support Systems

Classic AI bias ≠ generative bias.
Predictive models focus on input data; generative systems can produce biased or stereotyped content.

Generative outputs vary by who is described.
Wording, tone, and recommendations can shift based on identity cues.

Decision-support AI amplifies analyst assumptions.
Bias in inputs or framing leads to biased insights at scale.

Representational harms:
Certain groups are misrepresented, marginalised, or stereotyped.

Allocative harms:
Biased outputs can lead to unequal access to opportunities or resources.

Fairness requires active design choices.
It doesn't happen by default—build it in, measure it, and review it.

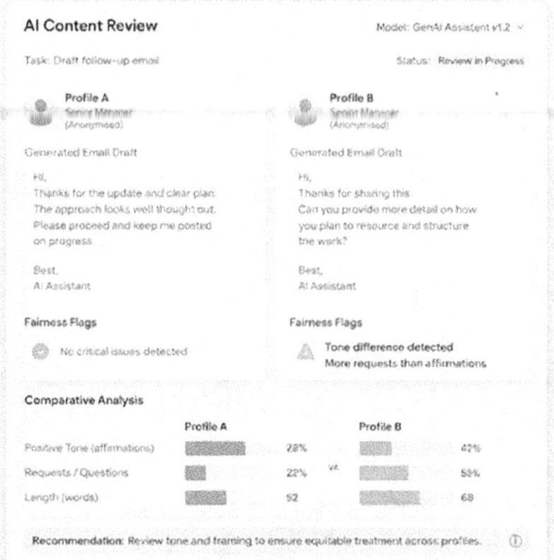

What you Need to Remember

Generative AI can produce plausible yet biased content. Fairness means ensuring outputs are respectful, accurate, and equitable—regardless of who is being described.

Harm can be representational (e.g., stereotypes, erasure, demeaning portrayals) or allocative (e.g., unequal opportunities, recommendations, or outcomes). Both matter.

Decision-support systems do not remove bias—they can scale it. The quality of inputs, prompts, and assumptions directly shapes the recommendations.

Fairness is a practice, not a setting.
Use diverse data, test across groups, monitor outputs, and be ready to adjust.

Design checkpoints: prompts, training data, evaluation groups

Questions to ask your AI tool

When to escalate to human review

Bias Testing and Red Teaming

1. Systematically probe models for unequal treatment of groups.
2. Use comparative prompts that only change demographic details, then compare tone and quality.
3. Run structured red-team exercises to surface harmful or unfair outputs before launch.
4. Maintain evaluation sets that cover common fairness-sensitive scenarios.
5. Involve human reviewers with relevant lived experience, and repeat tests whenever models, prompts, or use cases change.

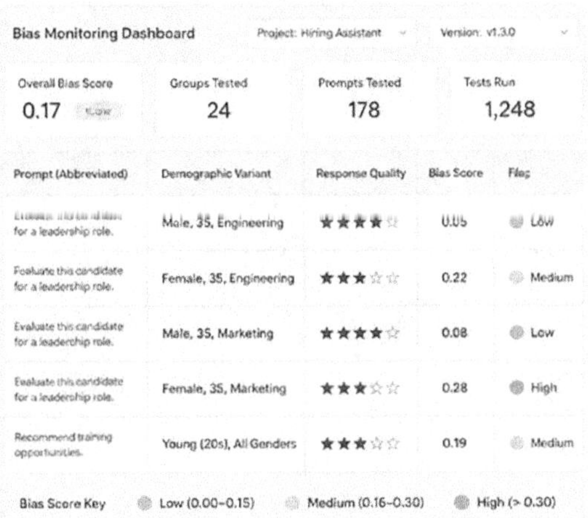

Bias Monitoring Dashboard Project: Hiring Assistant Version: v1.3.0

Overall Bias Score	Groups Tested	Prompts Tested	Tests Run
0.17 Low	24	178	1,248

Prompt (Abbreviated)	Demographic Variant	Response Quality	Bias Score	Flag
[illegible] for a leadership role.	Male, 35, Engineering	★★★★☆	0.05	Low
Evaluate this candidate for a leadership role.	Female, 35, Engineering	★★★☆☆	0.22	Medium
Evaluate this candidate for a leadership role.	Male, 35, Marketing	★★★★☆	0.08	Low
Evaluate this candidate for a leadership role.	Female, 35, Marketing	★★★☆☆	0.28	High
Recommend training opportunities.	Young (20s), All Genders	★★★☆☆	0.19	Medium

Bias Score Key: Low (0.00–0.15) Medium (0.16–0.30) High (> 0.30)

What you Need to Remember

Bias doesn't always show up on its own — you have to look for it. Deliberate bias testing helps uncover unequal treatment that can hide in plain sight.

Use comparative prompts that change only demographic details to spot differences in tone, quality, and outcomes across groups.

Run structured red-team exercises to provoke edge cases and surface harmful or unfair outputs before your system reaches real users.

Maintain and expand evaluation datasets that reflect fairness-sensitive scenarios relevant to your domain and population.

Involve human reviewers with relevant lived experience, and restart tests on every significant change to models, prompts, or use cases.

- New model version
- New prompt template
- New use case
- Unexpected user complaints

5.2 Bias, Fairness, and Inclusion in AI Use

Inclusive Design and Recourse

- Design AI to work fairly for everyone it will affect.
- Plan for language, literacy, accessibility and cultural differences.
- Explain: people should understand how AI influenced a decision.
- Challenge: give clear routes to question AI-informed outcomes.
- Remedy: have processes to fix unfair or incorrect decisions.
- Recourse is a legal obligation in many regulations.

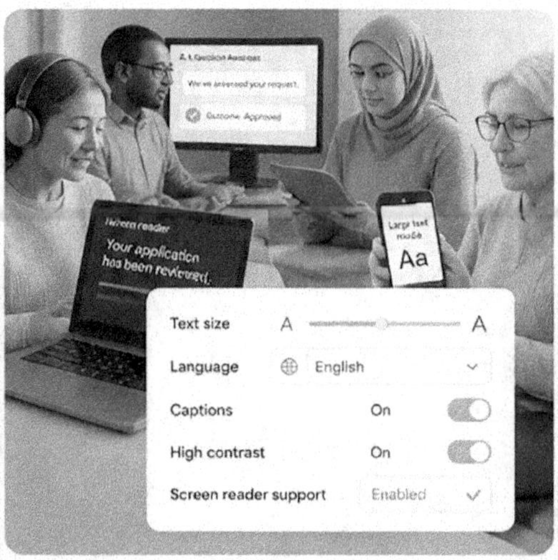

What you Need to Remember

Recourse has three pillars that build trust and ensure accountability.

Explanation: people are given clear, timely, and understandable reasons for an AI-influenced decision.

Challenge: people have an accessible way to question or dispute a decision and ask for a human review.

Remedy: when a decision is wrong or unfair, you fix the outcome and improve the systems to prevent it happening again.

Laws like the EU AI Act, GDPR and sector rules make recourse a legal requirement—not just a best practice.

AI decision review queue — All statuses

Decision	Explanation sent?	Challenge requested?	Status
Loan application ID: 78231	Yes 10 May 09:12	—	Closed 10 May
Job screening ID: 62419	Yes 9 May 14:45	Yes 10 May 10:02	Under review 10 May
Insurance claim ID: 99104	Yes 8 May 16:33	Yes 9 May 11:20	Remedy in progress 10 May
Credit limit ID: 55872	Yes 7 May 12:05	—	Closed 7 May
Service access ID: 44218	No —	Yes 9 May 09:17	Awaiting explanation
Account flag ID: 33081	Yes 6 May 08:50	No —	Pending

Design: involve diverse users early.

Document: log explanations and decisions.

Deliver recourse: clear contacts, timelines, ownership.

Explainability in LLM-Based Systems

Outputs come from weights, not rules.
LLMs generate responses from billions of learned parameters, not human-readable logic.

Mechanistic "why" is typically inaccessible.
We usually can't trace a single reason for a model's decision.

Post-hoc explanations are approximations.
Summaries, citations, and chain-of-thought provide helpful context, not guarantees of truth.

RAG improves transparency by surfacing sources.
Retrieval-augmented generation ground responses in external documents we can show.

Governance should match what can be explained.
Design policies and controls around realistic, verifiable forms of explainability.

Complex patterns, not step-by-step rules

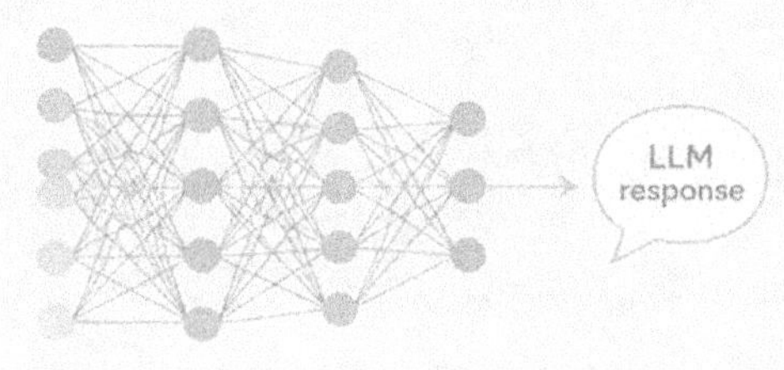

What you Need to Remember

LLM outputs are inherently hard to explain at a mechanistic level. Governance should focus on explainability we can realistically provide—such as sources, summaries, and documented limits.

Use retrieval-augmented generation and chain-of-thought explanations to increase transparency and build user trust.

Set policies that reflect known limits, require documentation of assumptions and sources, and escalate high-impact decisions for human review.

Good practice for AI explainability in LLM projects

- Record prompts & settings
- Log data sources
- Flag high-impact decisions
- Document known limits
- Offer user-facing notes

Confidence, Uncertainty, and Limitation Reporting

- Language models sound confident even when they're wrong.
- High-stakes use should require visible uncertainty and limitation notes.
- Use prompts like "List assumptions", "Flag low-confidence areas", "Note missing data".
- Read fluency critically — clear wording ≠ correct answer.
- Design outputs with confidence scores, sources, and warning flags.

Why it matters

AI systems can produce responses in a very confident tone even when the information is incomplete or incorrect.

Strong governance combines smart prompting with user training so teams question outputs, understand limits, and avoid over-reliance.

Structured confidence and limitation sections make the model's boundaries visible, enabling better decisions and reducing risk in real-world use.

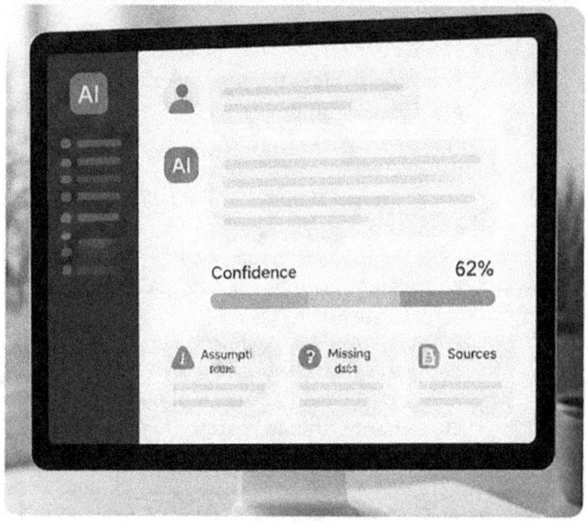

What you Need to Remember

- Models sound trustworthy regardless of accuracy.
- Always ask for assumptions, gaps, and missing data.
- Train users to interpret confidence indicators and warning flags.
- In high-risk settings, require structured confidence and sourcing sections.

When to insist on explicit uncertainty reporting:

- Regulatory decisions
- Financial approvals
- Medical or safety advice
- Automated customer decisions

Section 5: Governance of Generative AI Content and Decisions

5.3 Explainability and Decision Support

Decision Support vs Decision Making

1. Decision support:
AI surfaces options, evidence, and analysis — the human decides.

2. Decision making:
AI selects an outcome, takes an action, or issues a ruling — high governance risk.

3. Why the distinction matters
Legal, ethical, operational impact in HR, finance, healthcare, legal.

4. Policy requirement:
Each use case must state whether AI may support or decide.

5. Human-in-the-loop:
Where AI informs judgment, people must see its reasoning and can override.

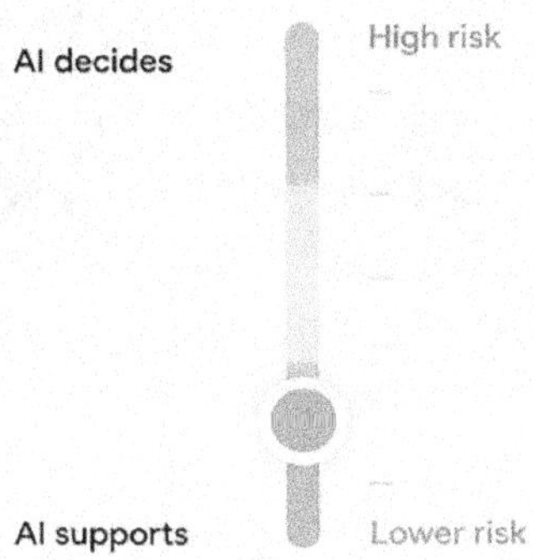

What you Need to Remember

Strong governance makes the line between decision support and decision making explicit.

Risk concentrates when AI is the decider in high-stakes areas like hiring, lending, triage, and legal assessment.

Policy must set this line for every use case and communicate it clearly.

Ensure humans truly understand AI contributions, review the rationale, and retain the power to override.

High impact on people	Regulated decisions	Limited ability to explain model	Little human oversight	Use of sensitive data

Documentation for High-Stakes Use

Keep a record for every high-stakes AI use: what was asked, what the AI produced, what the human decided.

Documentation enables audits, complaints handling, legal review, and incident investigations.

Always capture: input or prompt, AI output, human review notes, final decision, and decision-maker.

Store logs securely, follow retention policy, and make them available to oversight teams.

Without this trail, proving human accountability for AI-assisted decisions is almost impossible.

System Log

Search logs...

Date/Time	Case ID	Prompt	AI Output	Reviewer	Decision
May 22, 2025 09:14 AM	HR-2025-1478	Evaluate role fit for candidate	Candidate shows strong alignment with role...	HR Manager	Approved
May 22, 2025 10:32 AM	CR-2025-0856	Assess credit application	High risk detected due to payment history...	Credit Analyst	Declined
May 22, 2025 11:47 AM	HL-2025-2310	Prioritise care referral	Moderate risk, recommend further review...	Care Cocodinator	Escalated
May 22, 2025 02:18 PM	HR-2025-1489	Recommend promotion level	Meets criteria for senior level...	HR Director	Approved

Showing 1-4 of 4 results ‹ 1 ›

When AI influences decisions that affect people's jobs, finances, health, or rights, documentation turns intent into accountability.

A complete record shows what information was used, how the AI responded, how a human reviewed it, and why the final decision was made.

This evidence supports audits, regulatory reviews, and complaint handling—and helps your organisation learn from what happened.

Good documentation protects people, strengthens trust, and proves that humans remain in control of the outcomes that matter.

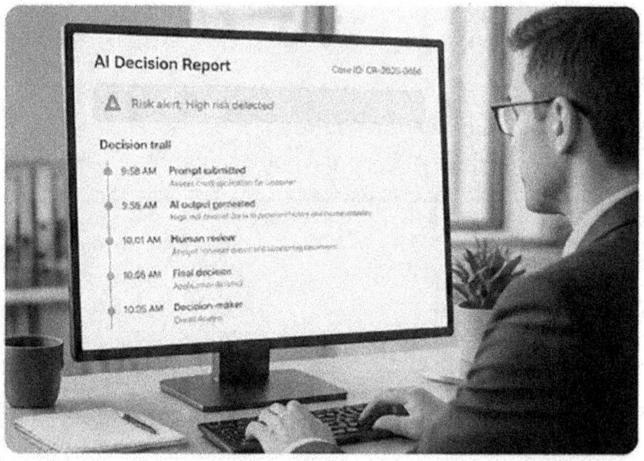

What you Need to Remember

- When AI affects jobs, money, health, or rights, documentation is a governance requirement.
- Capture the full chain: input, output, review, decision, decision-maker.
- This evidence is what shows accountable human oversight after the fact, especially in regulated sectors.

Protect people and organisation

Standardise how you log AI-assisted decisions

Make audits faster and fairer

SECTION 6

Operating AI Governance in the Enterprise

In this section, we look at how AI governance actually runs inside an enterprise: the bodies, roles, intake, everyday controls and incident management that turn principles into practice. We begin with structures and accountability: a dedicated AI steering group or risk committee rather than a bolted-on agenda item; distinct roles for legal, compliance, security, HR and IT; product and business owners as the accountable first line (if you deploy a use case, you own it); and the choice between federated and centralized governance.

We then cover intake and experimentation: use-case registration and triage that give governance visibility, risk scoring and proportionate approval routing so low-risk cases are not throttled, and sandboxes with strict data hygiene, treating the move from pilot to production as a genuine step-change. A block of everyday operating controls maps to real use: drafting and summarization, spreadsheet analysis, presentation creation, and research and retrieval, where verification must precede action or publication.

The largest part of the section is incident management. We define AI incidents and near misses (the latter being the canary in the coal mine) and set out what must be reported, to whom, and against which triggers (individual harm, potential data breach, safety-critical failure, regulatory or press exposure). Investigation and root-cause analysis group AI failures into prompt, data, tool and model categories, with immediate evidence preservation because logs and prompt histories expire quickly.

Corrective actions map directly onto those root causes, and learning loops feed findings back so the organisation measurably improves rather than fixing one thing at a time. Stakeholder communication and remediation are part of the governance response, not an afterthought: briefing leadership, legal and compliance quickly, and giving harmed individuals a way to challenge and be put right. Finally, an AI incident register provides a single, searchable record of what went wrong, why and what was done: enabling pattern-spotting and audit evidence.

Section 6: Operating AI Governance in the Enterprise

6.1 Corporate AI Governance Structures

AI Steering Groups and Committees

Create a named AI steering group with decision-making authority.

Include C-suite sponsor plus legal, risk, IT, HR and key business leads.

Give the group ownership of AI policy and the AI risk appetite statement.

Use a risk/ethics sub-committee for deep review of deployments and incidents.

Set clear mandate, quorum and escalation rules; meet monthly plus ad-hoc for urgent issues.

AI Governance Steering Group — Membership Matrix

Role	AI responsibilities
Chair (C-suite)	Sets direction, risk appetite and approves major AI decisions
Legal	Ensures compliance, privacy, and regulatory allynment
Risk	Owns AI risk framework, assessments and risk monitoring
IT	Responsible for platform security, data governance and operations
HR	Overeses workforce impact, training and responsible use
Business Units	Represents business needs, use cases and value delivery

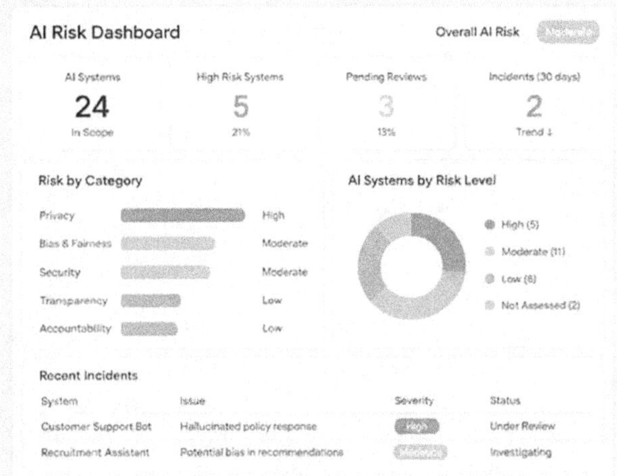

What you Need to Remember

Central AI governance starts with an empowered, accountable steering group. Membership must span the teams that carry AI risk. The group owns the AI risk appetite and policy. A smaller risk/ethics committee handles detailed reviews and incidents. Meet monthly, with ad-hoc sessions for urgent issues. A written mandate and clear escalation paths turn your group from a talking shop into real governance.

- What AI decisions need steering group approval?
- What are our top AI risks and current red flags?
- Who should be at the table—and who might be missing?
- How do we escalate AI issues and who decides?

Section 6: Operating AI Governance in the Enterprise

6.1 Corporate AI Governance Structures

Roles for Legal, Compliance, Security, HR, and IT

Shared accountability
AI governance is everyone's responsibility. Work together, stay aligned, and escalate early.

Legal
Ensure lawful use, review contracts and liability, and manage regulatory risk.

Compliance
Monitor regulations, maintain policies and records, and drive audit readiness.

Security
Protect data and systems, manage access, and reduce AI-related risks.

HR
Support responsible use, training, and workforce impact and change.

IT
Evaluate and implement tools, ensure integration, and maintain performance.

Named AI leads
Designate owners, define decision rights, and drive accountability.

AI Governance RACI Snapshot (Example)

AI Risk / Activity	Legal	Compliance	Security	HR	IT
Policy & Standards	C	A	C	C	C
Tool Evaluation	C	C	A	C	R
Data Privacy	A	C	R	I	C
Risk Assessment	C	A	R	C	C
User Training	I	C	C	A	R
Incident Response	C	C	A	I	R

R Responsible · A Accountable · C Consulted · I Informed

What you Need to Remember

Effective AI governance depends on collaboration across Legal, Compliance, Security, HR, and IT.

Each function has a distinct role, but decisions and oversight must be coordinated.

Define who owns decisions, how risks are assessed, and how issues are escalated.

Keep policies current, document actions, and review results regularly.

Strong governance builds trust, reduces risk, and enables responsible AI innovation.

- Agree who signs off AI use
- Log AI tool access
- Review policies every quarter
- Report issues and learn

Product and Business-Owner Responsibilities

- Central governance defines the rules; business owners apply them in daily operations.
- Each AI use case in a business unit has a named accountable owner.
- Owners register the use case, complete required risk assessments, and set up monitoring.
- They act as the first line of defence—spotting issues before they reach central governance.
- Product managers embedding AI into tools carry the same ownership duties.
- Clear ownership avoids the 'someone else will check it' failure mode.

What you Need to Remember

Central governance can set the framework, but it can't sit beside every user for every prompt, workflow, or deployment decision.

Business owners and product managers are the first line: if you deploy an AI use case, you own it—register it, assess the risks, and monitor it in life.

Because they are closest to the data, users, and context, they are best placed to spot failure modes early and prevent the 'nobody was watching' problem.

AI Use Case Registration

Business Unit	Select business unit
Use Case Name	Enter use case name
Owner	Select owner
Risk Tier	Select risk tier

- [ ] Monitoring Set Up
- [ ] Reviewed by Governance

Submit Registration

OWNERSHIP CHECKLIST

1. Register the AI use case
2. Complete risk assessment
3. Set up ongoing monitoring & escalation

Section 6: Operating AI Governance in the Enterprise

6.1 Corporate AI Governance Structures

Centralized Governance

Centralized Governance

- Decisions and standards set by a central authority.
- Ensures consistency, compliance, and risk control.
- Can be slower to adapt to local needs.

Federated Governance

- Business units have more autonomy within guardrails.
- Enables speed, innovation, and local relevance.
- Requires strong standards and oversight to manage risk.

Hybrid (Centre-of-Excellence) Model

- Central team sets policies, standards, and tools.
- Business units own execution within defined guardrails.
- Balances control with agility.

Escalation Paths

- Clear routes for raising and resolving issues.
- Ensures timely decisions for high-risk or ambiguous cases.

	Centralized	Federated
Consistency	High consistency across the enterprise	Varies by unit; greater local flexibility
Speed	Slower due to central approval	Faster local decision-making
Risk Enforcement	Stronger control and enforcement	Depends on unit maturity and oversight
Best For	High-risk use cases, regulated functions	Innovation, experimentation, and local solutions

What you Need to Remember

Centralized governance maximizes consistency and control but can slow innovation. Federated governance enables speed and local relevance but requires strong guardrails and oversight.

Most organizations succeed with a hybrid centre-of-excellence model: a central team sets standards, provides tools and guidance, and partners with business units to execute responsibly.

Clear escalation paths ensure high-risk or uncertain cases get the right attention quickly. Define triggers, owners, and response times—and communicate them widely.

Ask: Who owns final sign-off for high-risk AI?

Have we documented our escalation path?

Are standards applied consistently across units?

Do teams know where to go for guidance?

Use-Case Registration and Triage

Register every AI idea
Every proposed AI use case is logged before work begins.

Capture the 4 basics
Purpose, data involved, intended users, and likely impact.

Triage the request
Decide if it needs light-touch sign-off or full review.

Use a simple intake form
Avoid ad-hoc tool adoption that bypasses oversight.

Registration is the on-ramp
It's how teams access governance support and tooling.

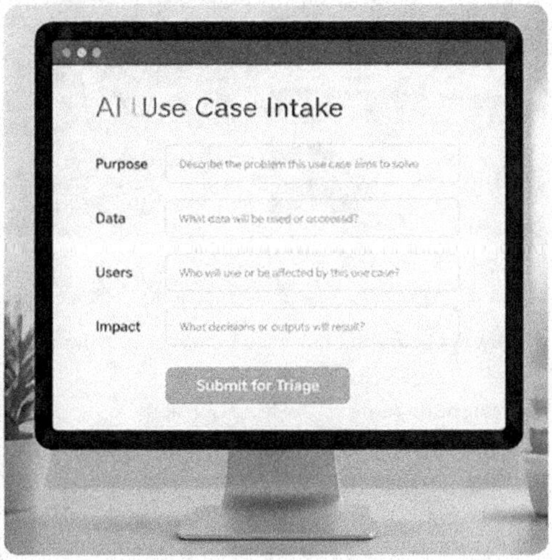

What you Need to Remember

Registration is the first step in a healthy AI intake process. As soon as someone says 'we want to use AI for this', that intention should be captured somewhere official. Before anything is built or trialled, registration creates visibility so governance isn't chasing tools already in use.

Good registrations cover four things: what problem is being solved, what data the AI will touch, who will use or be affected by it, and what decisions or outputs will result.

Triage then applies a quick filter – is this a low-risk request that needs a five-minute check, or something that requires a deeper review panel?

The cultural message: registration isn't gatekeeping. It's how governance teams know where to focus support, standards, and resources.

When to register
New AI tools, projects, or automations

Who to involve
Business owner + data / risk leads

Where to log it
Single, approved registry or intake form

Risk Scoring and Approval Routing

- Different AI use cases carry different levels of risk.
- Score risk by data sensitivity, decision impact, automation level, and scale.
- Low-risk use cases (e.g. internal drafting) follow a fast-track path.
- Medium / high-risk use cases route to legal, compliance, security or an AI committee.
- Criteria must be documented, consistent, and regularly reviewed.

AI Use Case Risk Dashboard

Search use cases... All statuses

Use Case	Data Sensitivity	Decision Impact	Automation Level	Scale (People Affected)	Risk Score	Risk Level	Route
Internal memo drafting	Low	Low	Low	< 50	15 / 100	[illegible]	Line Manager Sign-off
Customer email replies	Medium	Low	Medium	50 – 500	38 / 100	Medium	Line Manager Sign-off
Fraud alerts	High	High	High	5,000+	78 / 100	[illegible]	Compliance Review
Hiring shortlist	High	High	Medium	100 – 1,000	72 / 100	[illegible]	AI Committee Review

Scores are indicative. Review details and documentation for full context.

Risk scoring keeps intake proportionate so simple use cases are not slowed down.

The model looks at data sensitivity, how directly AI informs decisions, how much human review is in the loop, and how many people are affected.

Internal drafting sits at the low end of the scale; screening job applications or fraud detection sit at the high end.

Routing logic sends low-risk use cases to line-manager sign-off and higher-risk use cases to legal, compliance, security, or a formal AI review group.

The key principle is consistent treatment of similar use cases.

What you Need to Remember

- Always score the use case before approving.
- Match the route to the level of risk.
- Keep criteria stable and documented.
- Treat similar use cases the same way.

1. Intake → Risk Score → Route

Intake → Risk Score → Route

2. Risk Level Legend

- Low Risk
- Medium Risk
- High Risk

3. Keep it Up to Date

Update your scoring model as regulations and business risks evolve.

Sandboxes and Controlled Experimentation

Safe test space before production.
Run experiments in an isolated environment before any real-world deployment.

Only synthetic or anonymised data.
Protect privacy by using synthetic datasets or fully anonymised data in all sandbox tests.

Limited access to named participants.
Restrict sandbox access to approved users with clear roles and responsibilities.

Capture results and risks and send back to governance.
Document outcomes, metrics, and risks; escalate findings to the governance body for review.

Experiments are time-boxed with clear end date.
Define start and end dates to ensure focus, accountability, and review.

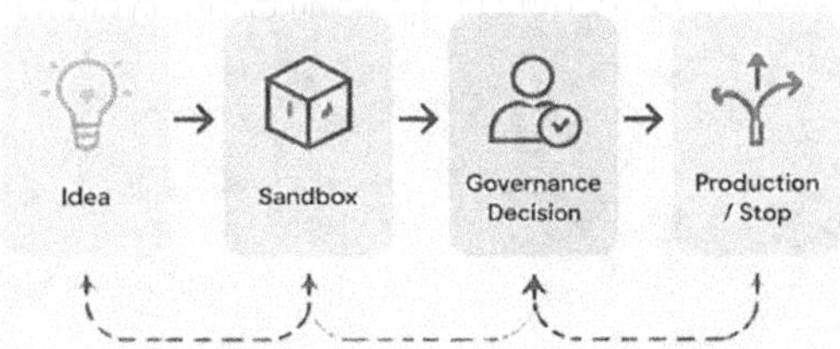

Learnings and risks flow back to improve future ideas

What you Need to Remember

Sandboxes let your team explore AI ideas safely without exposing real data or operations.

Strong guardrails—clean data, limited access, and clear responsibilities—reduce risk while encouraging innovation.

Capture results, monitor risks, and report back to governance so informed decisions guide what moves forward.

Time-box every experiment to maintain focus, ensure accountability, and avoid drift.

Responsible experimentation builds trust today and better AI outcomes tomorrow.

Use a Sandbox When...

1. Testing new AI tools
2. Unsure about data risks
3. Exploring edge cases
4. Validating controls before rollout

Moving from Pilot to Production

From pilot success... to production readiness

- Pilot results alone don't justify scaling.
- Show evidence of stability, safety and oversight before go-live.
- Have human review workflows defined and owners named.
- Set up monitoring for drift, errors and unusual outputs.
- Document a clear rollback / shutdown plan.
- Refresh governance docs to describe the production system, not just the experiment.

AI Deployment Readiness Checklist

Checklist Item	Status
Human review defined	Complete
Monitoring configured	[illegible]
Risk assessment updated	Complete
Rollback plan documented	Complete
Stakeholder sign-off recorded	In progress
Governance record updated	Not started

What you Need to Remember

Pilot and production are different risk environments. Pilots run with small, supervised groups; production exposes real customers, live data and less hands-on oversight.

Before scaling, confirm that human review steps are embedded in workflows, monitoring can flag performance drift or harmful outputs, and there is a tested rollback path.

Treat stakeholder sign-off as a new approval for the higher-risk setting, and update your governance record so the production system is documented as its own, traceable artifact.

Quick Governance Check Before You Scale

- Scope changed?
- New user groups?
- Data risk higher?
- Controls tested?
- Rollback rehearsed?

Drafting and Summarization Controls | Email, reports, and meeting notes

AI-assisted drafting is now among the most common everyday workplace activities.

Email, reports, and meeting summaries all carry different confidentiality and accuracy risks.

Controls focus on three areas: what goes in, what comes out, and who reviews it before it is sent or filed.

Input controls: avoid pasting confidential data, personal information, or client-identifiable content into external AI tools.

Output controls: treat AI-generated drafts as a starting point, not a finished product — check facts, tone, and attributions.

Review gates: for external communications and formal reports, a human should confirm accuracy and appropriate disclosure before sending.

Meeting note risks: AI summaries may misattribute statements, omit nuance, or include sensitive discussion — always review before distributing.

From Draft to Send: The Control Flow

1. **Input** — Check what you share with AI. Remove sensitive or identifying data.
2. **Draft** — Use AI to draft or summarize content.
3. **Review** — Check accuracy, tone, attributions, and completeness.
4. **Approve & Send** — Human confirms and approves before sending or filing.

What you Need to Remember

This slide covers the controls that should be in place when AI is helping people draft or summarize — which by now is something most teams do every day.

AI-assisted drafting is already widespread — email replies, weekly reports, meeting recaps — so this is high-frequency, everyday risk, not an edge case. Different formats carry different risks: a meeting summary shared with external parties is far more sensitive than an internal draft email. So controls need to fit the context, not just apply a blanket rule.

The three control areas are inputs, outputs, and review. On inputs, the key discipline is not pasting in content that shouldn't be in an external AI system — things like client names, personal data, or confidential project details.

On outputs, the point is that AI drafts need a human pass — checking for accuracy, appropriate tone, and anything that was hallucinated or wrongly inferred.

And for anything going outside the team, there should be a clear review gate before it leaves.

Meeting notes deserve a specific mention because they feel low-stakes but often aren't — a misattributed comment or a dropped nuance in a sensitive discussion can cause real problems, especially if the summary is widely shared.

Key Principles for Responsible Drafting

- Protect sensitive information at the input.
- Validate AI output — don't trust blindly.
- Human review is mandatory for external communications.
- Be extra careful with meeting notes and summaries.
- Context matters — apply the right controls for the right risk.

Spreadsheet and Data Analysis Controls | Formula generation, interpretation, and model risk

AI tools like Copilot in Excel can generate formulas, write analysis, and interpret data — quickly and with errors that are easy to miss.

Formula risk: AI-generated formulas may look correct but contain logic errors, incorrect ranges, or wrong assumptions.

Interpretation risk: AI narrative summaries of data can misstate trends, omit outliers, or draw unsupported conclusions.

Model risk: in financial or operational spreadsheets, unreviewed AI changes can propagate errors at scale.

Control principle: treat AI-generated spreadsheet content as a draft — verify formulas, check calculations, and validate key outputs manually.

High-stakes use: spreadsheets used for budgets, forecasts, or decisions must have a named human owner who signs off before use.

Version control: save before applying AI changes so you can compare and roll back if needed.

AI Spreadsheet Verification Checklist

Check	What to Verify	✓ Done
Formulas	Logic, ranges, references, and assumptions	☐
Calculations	Key outputs and totals recalculate correctly	☐
Data	Source data, filters, and date ranges	☐
Interpretation	Narrative matches the data; outliers and exceptions acknowledged	☐
Sign-off	Named owner reviewed and approved	☐

What you Need to Remember

Spreadsheets are one of the most formula-driven, consequential artifacts in any business, and AI tools are now deeply embedded in how people work with them. This slide is about where that combination creates risk and what the controls look like.

The speed of AI formula generation is exactly what makes it risky — it's easy to accept a plausible-looking result without checking the underlying logic. Formula errors are a classic example: a range that's one row off, or an IF condition that doesn't match the intent — these are hard to spot on visual inspection.

AI narrative interpretation introduces a different kind of risk: the summary might say "sales are trending up" when the data is more mixed — and if that narrative gets shared, the error travels with it.

Model risk is the amplified version of this — in a spreadsheet that feeds a budget model or a pricing tool, one wrong AI-generated formula can cascade. The control here is treating AI output as a draft and verifying key cells and outputs, not just the formula syntax.

For anything that informs a real decision, there needs to be a named person who's reviewed it and is accountable for it. And the version control point is practical habit: save a copy before letting AI make changes, so there's always a clean rollback point.

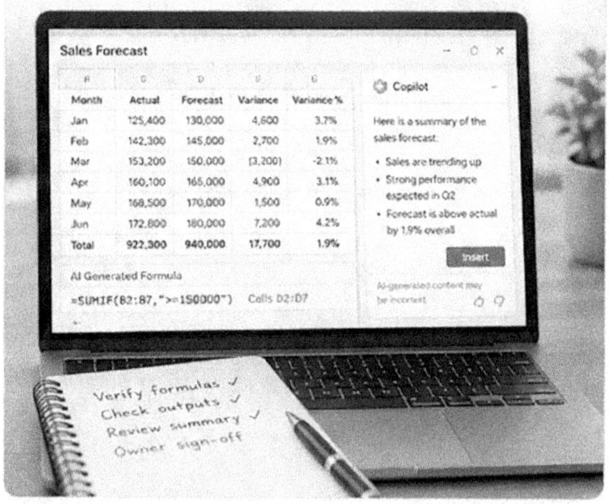

Key Controls for Spreadsheet and Data Analysis

- Treat AI output as a draft — always verify.
- Check formulas, calculations, and assumptions.
- Validate key outputs and data sources manually.
- Named owner reviews and signs off.
- Save before AI changes to enable rollback and auditability.

Presentation and Document Creation Controls | Accuracy, confidentiality, and brand consistency

AI can generate entire presentations and documents from a prompt or source material — fast, but with significant quality and risk variation.

Accuracy risk: AI may invent statistics, misquote sources, or present outdated information with false confidence.

Confidentiality risk: source documents used as AI input may contain information not intended for the output audience.

Brand risk: AI-generated content may not reflect approved messaging, current terminology, or visual standards.

Control: fact-check all statistics and claims against primary sources before presenting or publishing.

Control: review source material before uploading — strip or redact content that shouldn't inform the output.

Control: pass AI-generated documents through a brand or communications review for external and formal internal use.

From Input to Audience: Apply the Controls

1. **Prepare Input** — Review source material and remove sensitive information.
2. **Generate** — Use AI to draft slides or documents.
3. **Verify** — Fact-check claims, statistics, and sources.
4. **Brand Review** — Ensure accuracy of messaging, tone, and visuals.
5. **Publish** — Human approval before sharing or presenting.

What you Need to Remember

This slide addresses a scenario that's increasingly common: someone drops a brief or a few documents into an AI tool and asks it to produce a slide deck or a report. The output can look polished and complete — and that's part of the problem.

The accuracy risk is real and specific: AI tools regularly invent plausible-sounding statistics, get dates or names slightly wrong, or present information from an earlier version of a dataset. The fact-check control isn't optional — any figure or claim that will be presented to an audience or used in a decision needs to be traced back to a reliable source.

Confidentiality risk comes from the input side: if someone uploads an internal strategy document to generate a client-facing summary, they may inadvertently allow sensitive information to shape or even appear in the output. The habit of reviewing what goes in — not just what comes out — is an important discipline.

Brand risk is subtler but organizationally important: AI-generated content tends to be generic, may use outdated product names or discontinued messaging, and often doesn't match an organization's tone or visual standards. For anything going externally, a communications or brand review step is appropriate.

Key Controls for Responsible Presentations and Documents

- Verify all facts, figures, and attributions.
- Protect confidential information in inputs and outputs.
- Align with brand voice, messaging, and visual standards.
- Human review required before sharing.
- Maintain versions to compare and roll back if needed.

Search, Research, and Knowledge Retrieval Controls | Verification before action or publication

AI is increasingly used to answer research questions, find information, and synthesize knowledge across sources.

Retrieval-augmented systems can ground responses in real documents — but still introduce errors through misreading, omission, or outdated sources.

Hallucination risk: AI may generate confident-sounding responses with no reliable source behind them.

Source quality risk: AI may retrieve or cite low-quality, biased, or out-of-date information without flagging it.

Control: always ask the AI to cite its sources, then verify those sources directly — do not rely on the AI's summary alone.

Control: apply a "verify before act" principle — no AI research output should be acted on or published without human cross-check.

Control: for regulatory, legal, medical, or financial topics, use AI to assist the search — not to replace expert review.

Verify Before Act — Simple Workflow

1. **Ask** — Request sources for the answer
→ 2. **Check** — Go to the original sources
→ 3. **Verify** — Confirm facts, dates and context
→ 4. **Act** — Use only when human-verified

What you Need to Remember

AI tools are now commonly used as a first port of call for research — internal knowledge retrieval, market context, regulatory lookups, competitive intelligence. This slide is about where that creates risk and what responsible practice looks like.

Even retrieval-augmented systems — the ones that pull from a defined knowledge base — can misread documents, omit key qualifications, or surface an older version of a policy. And with general-purpose AI, hallucination is a live risk: the model produces a confident, well-structured answer that simply isn't accurate, with a fabricated source to back it up. Source quality is a related concern — AI doesn't automatically distinguish between a peer-reviewed paper and an opinion piece, or between current guidance and superseded regulation.

The "cite and verify" control is a practical discipline: always ask the AI to tell you where its answer comes from, then go to that source directly rather than trusting the paraphrase. The "verify before act" principle extends that — any research output that will drive a decision, inform client advice, or go into a published document should be cross-checked by a human before it's used.

And for high-stakes domains — legal, medical, financial, regulatory — the AI should be framing the question and narrowing the search space, not providing the final answer.

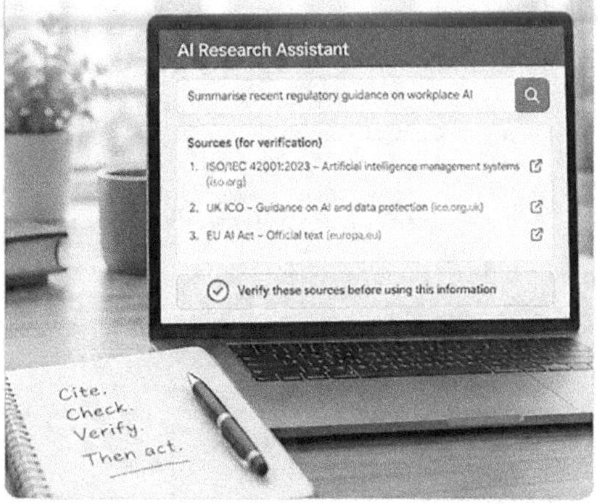

Key Checks for Responsible AI Research

- Always request and review sources
- Check authority, date and relevance
- Verify facts before decision or publication
- Use AI to assist — not replace expert review
- Apply stricter checking for legal, medical and financial topics

Defining AI Incidents and Near Misses

- **Define an AI incident as:** AI causes harm, produces a materially wrong output, or breaches policy/law.

Define a near miss as: could have caused harm but didn't — still needs attention.

Examples include:

- System shares a hallucinated statistic with a client.
- AI summary exposes a confidential file or sensitive data.
- AI agent takes an unintended action or recommendation.

The threshold for incident status is based on impact on people, business, or compliance.

Clear definitions prevent under-reporting and trigger the right response.

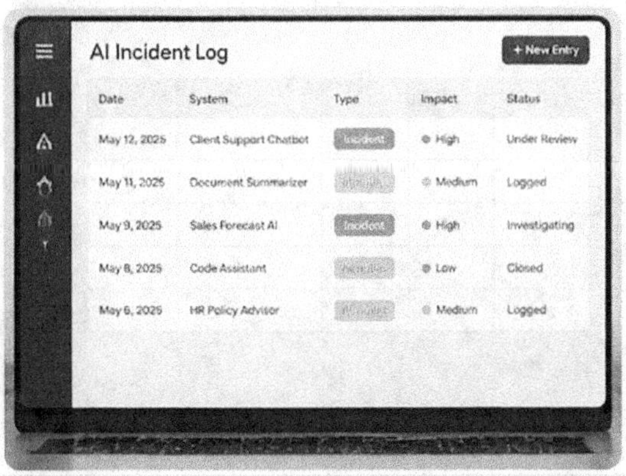

What you Need to Remember

We're managing events where AI causes real harm, produces significantly wrong output, or breaks a policy or legal rule.

Near misses are early warning signals that controls are weak.

For example, a chatbot might invent a statistic and send it to a client. Or an AI agent might access a restricted file during a task.

We need agreed criteria so teams don't over-report noise or under-report real problems. Clear definitions make the whole incident process work.

Did the AI output create or risk real harm?

Was any policy, legal, or data protection rule at risk?

Would you be comfortable if this outcome were on the front page?

If in doubt, log it as a near miss.

Section 6: Operating AI Governance in the Enterprise

6.4 Incident Management for AI Failures

What Must Be Reported

Policy-defined triggers:
harm to individuals, regulatory breach, data exposure, reputational impact

Employee-facing AI:
bias, incorrect decisions, or unsanctioned personal data use

Customer-facing AI:
misleading outputs, failed safety filters, or unauthorized disclosure

Agentic systems:
unintended actions, scope violations, or failure to escalate to a human

Near misses:
report without blame to surface early warning signals

Regulatory duties:
some incidents must be reported externally (e.g. GDPR, sector AI rules)

AI Incident Log

Date	System Type	Trigger Category	Status
May 8, 2025	Employee Tool	Bias / Incorrect Decision	Under Review
May 7, 2025	Customer Chatbot	Data Exposure / Disclosure Attempt	Open
May 6, 2025	Agentic Workflow	Unintended Action / Scope Violation	Investigating
May 5, 2025	Employee Tool	Policy Breach / Unsanctioned Use	Closed

What you Need to Remember

Everyone must know **what counts as a reportable AI incident** and **who to tell.** If in doubt, report it.

AI systems differ: employee-facing tools, customer-facing services, and agentic systems carry different risks and reporting nuances.

A no-blame culture saves time and prevents harm. Report near misses openly so we can fix issues before they impact people or our business.

External reporting deadlines are tight. Data incidents and certain AI events may have strict legal or regulatory timeframes—early reporting ensures we meet our obligations.

If you spot an AI incident

1. **Capture** what happened →
2. **Classify** the system and trigger →
3. **Report** via the agreed channel

Investigation and Root-Cause Analysis

Prompt failure

Ambiguous, manipulated, or out-of-scope prompts drive unreliable responses.

Data failure

Stale, wrong, or sensitive data used—or data accessed that shouldn't be.

Tool / system failure

Integrations, plugins, or agents act outside their sanctioned scope.

Process failure

Human checks rushed or skipped; governance steps not followed.

Incident logged → Classify failure type → Capture evidence → Agree actions

What you Need to Remember

After an AI incident is logged, the investigation phase aims to find root cause, not blame.

Most issues fall into four buckets: prompt, data, tool/system, or process.

Walk through each in turn: What was asked? What data was used or exposed? What did connected tools do? Which human checks ran or failed?

Clear classification shapes fixes, accountability, and future controls.

- Capture evidence early (screens, logs, prompts, outputs).
- Tag incidents by failure type to spot patterns.
- Feed lessons into prompts, data quality checks, and process updates.

Running an Effective AI Incident Investigation

Preserve evidence immediately – prompts, outputs, logs, tool-use records.

Map the timeline – AI used, decision made, problem discovered.

Interview people involved – focus on what they knew, not blame.

Reproduce the issue safely to confirm likely root cause.

Record everything in a structured incident report, not email threads.

Separate facts from assumptions so the record stands up to review.

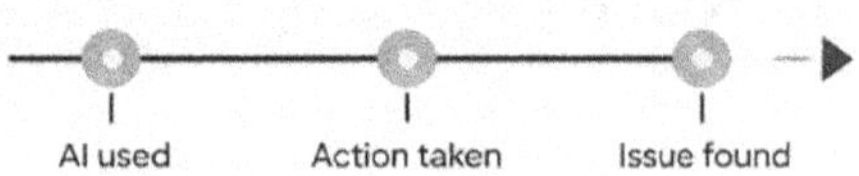

What you Need to Remember

Act fast to preserve evidence. Logs, prompts, outputs, and tool-use records can be overwritten or lost quickly.

Build a clear timeline of what happened—from when AI was used, to the decision taken, to when the issue was discovered.

Talk to the people involved. Focus on what they knew and did, not on blame.

Reproduce the failure in a safe environment if possible. This helps confirm the likely root cause and rules out guesswork.

Keep a factual, structured record of evidence, findings, and decisions. A good record supports learning and stands up to regulatory or legal scrutiny.

Before you start secure access & preserve logs.

During capture facts, decisions, and context.

After agree follow-up actions and controls.

Corrective Actions and Control Improvements

Design the right fixes

- Fix root causes, not surface symptoms.
- Prompt-level fixes: better templates, constrained inputs, banned patterns.
- Data-level fixes: tighter access, quality checks, narrower retrieval.
- Tool and agent fixes: reduced scope, extra approvals, limit risky integrations.
- Process fixes: clearer reviews, retraining, mandatory sign-off.
- Track every action to closure with an owner and deadline.

From incident to corrective actions

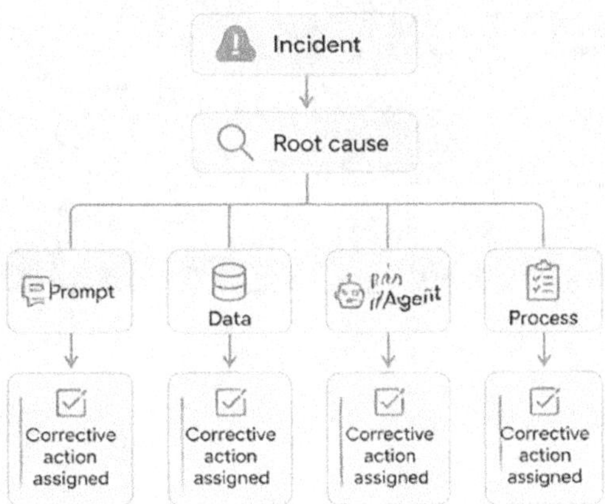

What you Need to Remember

Incident response only creates value when it leads to real improvement.

Match fixes directly to root causes across four categories: prompt, data, tool/agent, and process.

Turn insights into accountable actions — every item needs an owner, a deadline, and verification.

This discipline turns incidents into learning engine for safer, more trustworthy AI.

Log the incident → Capture root cause → Choose fix type → Assign owner & due date → Verify and close

6.4 Incident Management for AI Failures

Learning Loops After Incidents

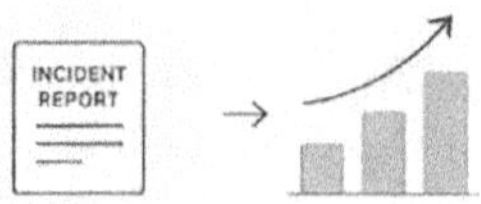

One review = one fix. Learning loops compound improvements.

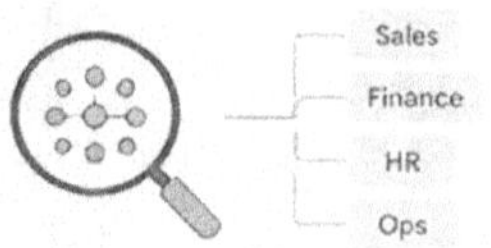

Spot patterns: repeated root causes or business units.

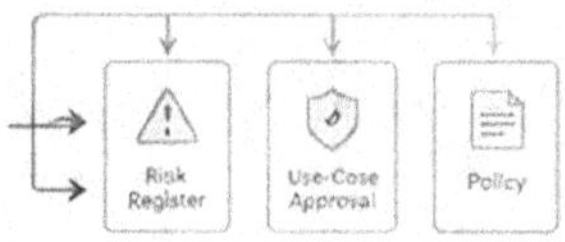

Feed insights into governance documents.

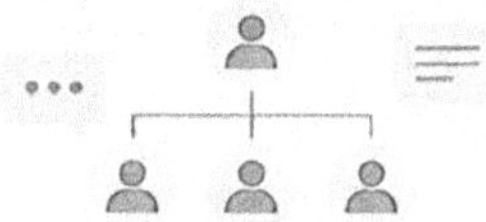

Share anonymised lessons across teams.

Schedule reviews of closed incidents: did controls hold?

Maturity grows when incident data shapes decisions.

What you Need to Remember

Strong AI governance doesn't end with responding to incidents—it improves because of them. Closing the loop means turning every incident into insight, and every insight into stronger systems, policies, and behaviours.

When lessons are captured, shared, and acted on, your organisation builds trust, reduces risk, and advances responsible AI—together.

Close the Loop

Update Governance

- ☑ Risk Register
- ☑ Standards
- ☑ Training

Share & Track

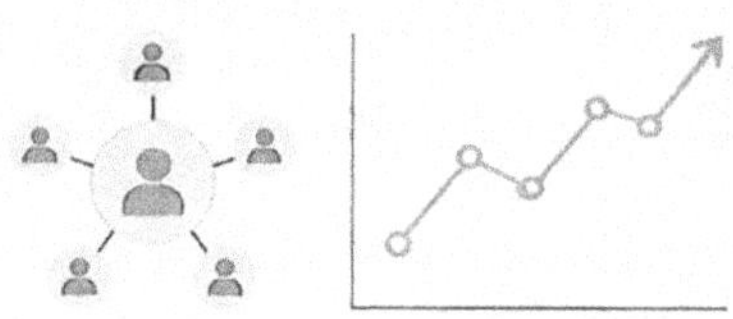

Stakeholder Communication and Remediation

1. Treat incident communication as a governance duty — not optional PR.
2. Brief leadership, legal, compliance and system owners quickly with accurate facts.
3. Notify impacted people where harm, bias or data exposure occurs — legal as well as ethical duty.
4. Follow any AI or data-protection rules that require regulator notification within set timeframes.
5. Where AI failures affect clients or partners, consider both contract terms and relationship impact.

Incident Communication Map

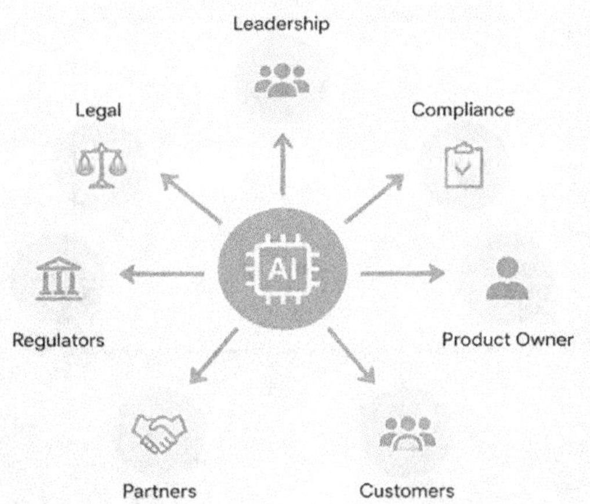

What you Need to Remember

When an AI system fails, communication is part of the governance response.

Brief the right internal teams fast.

If individuals are harmed or their data is exposed, they may have a legal right to be told.

Many regimes set clocks on regulator notification (for example 72 hours for some data breaches).

For clients and partners, think about contractual duties and trust.

Keep every message factual and measured: what happened, what you're doing, and what's still unknown — avoid speculation or premature conclusions.

- Agree who owns incident communication before you deploy.
- Maintain up-to-date contact lists for all stakeholder groups.
- Prepare notification templates for customers, regulators, and partners.
- Decide escalation thresholds for when to inform whom.
- Log every decision and message for audit and learning.

Managing Internal and External Consequences

Make things right for people, systems, and processes.

For individuals: fix wrong decisions, restore access, explain clearly, offer appeal routes.

For AI systems: decide whether to pause, restrict, or retire while risks are reviewed.

For the organisation: update policy, retrain staff, close governance gaps.

Document every step as carefully as the investigation — this is your evidence.

Handled well, an incident can signal governance maturity, not just failure.

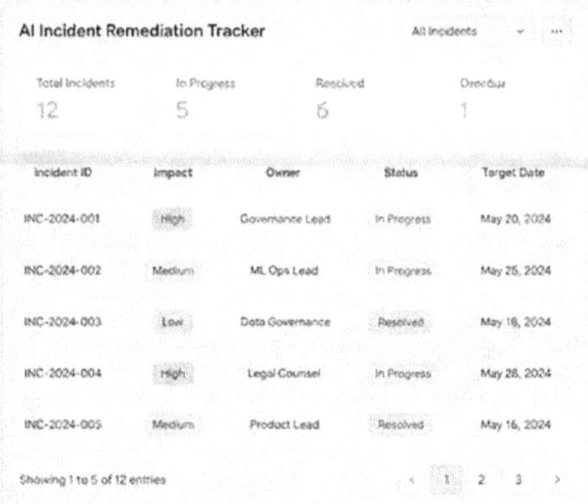

AI Incident Remediation Tracker

All Incidents

Total Incidents	In Progress	Resolved	Overdue
12	5	6	1

Incident ID	Impact	Owner	Status	Target Date
INC-2024-001	High	Governance Lead	In Progress	May 20, 2024
INC-2024-002	Medium	ML Ops Lead	In Progress	May 25, 2024
INC-2024-003	Low	Data Governance	Resolved	May 18, 2024
INC-2024-004	High	Legal Counsel	In Progress	May 28, 2024
INC-2024-005	Medium	Product Lead	Resolved	May 16, 2024

Showing 1 to 5 of 12 entries

AI incidents don't end when the immediate problem is contained. True remediation means making things right for the people affected, addressing risks in the AI system, and strengthening the organisation to prevent a recurrence.

For individuals, this may mean correcting decisions, restoring access, providing clear explanations, and offering fair appeal options.

For the AI system, it may mean pausing, restricting, or retiring the model while risks are reviewed. For the organisation, it means updating policies, retraining people, and closing governance gaps.

What you Need to Remember

Remediation is about restoring trust and reducing future harm. It requires clear actions across people, systems, and the organisation — and complete documentation of every decision and step.

Well-managed remediation shows accountability, strengthens confidence, and turns an incident into an opportunity to improve.

When to trigger remediation: harmed individuals or rights impacted.

When to review the AI system: new risks or repeated incidents.

When to escalate: regulator, client, or legal interest.

Section 6: Operating AI Governance in the Enterprise

6.4 Incident Management for AI Failures

Building an Incident Register

- Central log of AI incidents and near misses — kept in one place, not in emails.
- Capture key fields: date, system, incident type, root-cause category, impact level, actions, owner, closure status.
- Use the structure to spot patterns — repeated fields highlight systemic issues.
- Acts as audit evidence that AI governance is active and monitored.
- Review the register regularly at governance committee level, not just by the tech team.

Date	System	Incident Type	Root Cause	Impact	Owner	Status
2024-05-20	Model A	Biased Output	Training Data	High	J. Patel	[illegible]
2024-05-18	Chatbot	Incorrect Info	Prompt Design	Medium	M. Chen	[illegible]
2024-05-12	Credit Model	Model Drift	Data Drift	High	S. Khan	[illegible]
2024-05-08	Rec Engine	Outage	Service Failure	High	D. Lee	[illegible]
2024-04-30	Fraud Model	False Positive	Threshold Setting	Low	A. Singh	[illegible]

What you Need to Remember

Treat the incident register as the operational backbone of AI governance. A single, searchable log shows what went wrong, why, and what was done about it.

Structured fields make it possible to detect patterns, track actions to closure, and give regulators or auditors concrete evidence of control.

When a governance committee regularly reviews a current, well-maintained register, it signals a mature, accountable AI programme — far more convincing than a policy document that has never been tested by real incidents.

When to log: any AI error, bias, outage, or user complaint with impact.

Check quality: are root causes clear and actions assigned?

Use it: bring the register to every governance or risk meeting.

SECTION 7

Sector-Specific AI Governance Applications

In this section, we look at how AI governance plays out in specific sectors, where general principles meet concrete regulatory obligations and the stakes of getting it wrong are high. We begin with healthcare: the line between clinical support and clinical decision making, with obligations rising sharply along that spectrum; the highest protection for patient data under GDPR and HIPAA, rules written for databases rather than chat interfaces; lower-risk documentation and triage uses; and clinical accountability that cannot be delegated to an AI.

We then turn to financial services: customer-facing AI for lending and pricing treated as high-risk; spreadsheet and analyst workflows raising model-risk concerns, since Excel underpins P&L and capital models; the fraud sensitivity trade-off, where flagging more catches more legitimate activity too; and auditability, since 'the model decided' is not an acceptable answer to a regulator. Public services receive close attention because a public body is accountable for how outputs are reached: decisions on benefits, permits and school places; surveillance and profiling risks such as predictive policing; education and assessment; and accessibility for users a public service cannot choose.

Finally, corporate and professional services: choosing between ChatGPT, Claude and Copilot as a governance act; the tension between speed and the verification professional standards demand; over-permissioned connectors in knowledge management, since an agent inherits its setter's access; and billing, accountability and client transparency questions in law, accounting and consulting.

7.1 Healthcare and Life Sciences

Clinical Support vs Clinical Decision Making

Where AI Fits in Clinical Workflows

- AI spans a spectrum – from information lookup to treatment recommendations.
- Clinical support tools: surface evidence, summarise notes, flag interactions.
- Clinical decision tools: propose diagnoses, suggest treatments, plan care pathways.
- Governance boundary: informing clinicians vs replacing clinical judgement.
- Decision-making AI is usually regulated as a medical device (e.g. MDR, FDA).
- Each AI use case must be clearly documented and classified.

AI Use Spectrum in Clinical Workflows

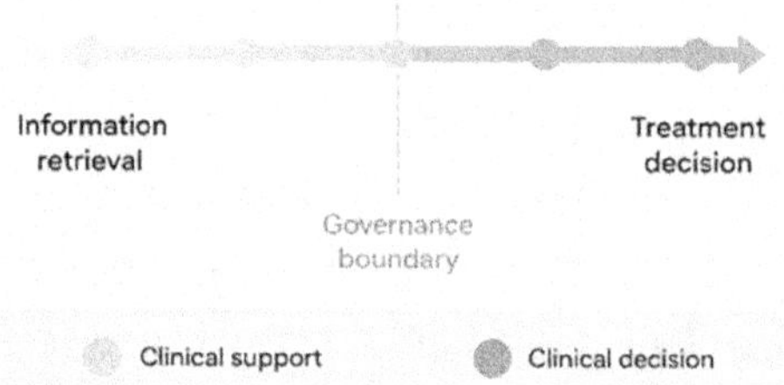

What you Need to Remember

AI tools in clinics range from simple support to direct decision-making. Support tools lighten workload and surface what humans might miss; decision tools generate recommendations that directly shape care.

This line matters for governance because regulators treat decision-making systems as medical devices with stricter approval, monitoring and liability rules.

Organisations should keep an up-to-date register of AI tools, showing where each sits on thie spectrum and revisiting that classification whenever capabilities change.

Ask if it's support or decision-making
Clarify how the tool influences diagnosis or treatment.

Check the regulatory status
Is it classified and approved as a medical device where required?

Document ownership
Record who is accountable for monitoring performance and risk.

Section 7: Sector-Specific AI Governance Applications

7.1 Healthcare and Life Sciences

Patient Data and Privacy Constraints

Protect patient identifiers
Never include names, MRNs, dates of birth, or other direct identifiers in prompts or outputs.

Respect data residency
Store and process patient data in approved regions only. Confirm where data is hosted and processed by your AI tools.

Minimise data exposure
Share only the minimum data necessary for the task. Remove or mask sensitive fields before use.

Use approved, vetted tools
Only use AI tools that have completed security, privacy, and compliance assessments.

Follow consent and legal rules
Ensure data use aligns with patient consent, privacy laws, and organisational policies.

Understand data flow
Know how data moves between your organisation and AI vendors — and where it is stored.

What you Need to Remember

Patient trust depends on how we protect their data. AI tools are powerful, but they must be used responsibly and within clear governance guardrails.

Always remove or mask identifiers, use approved tools, and respect data residency and consent requirements. When in doubt, don't include it.

Strong AI governance isn't about slowing down innovation — it's about ensuring safe, ethical, and lawful use of AI that protects patients and strengthens our organisation.

- Govern prompts, Not just databases
- Use de-identified data by default
- Lock down vendor data processing
- Log and audit AI use

Section 7: Sector-Specific AI Governance Applications

7.1 Healthcare and Life Sciences

Documentation, Communication, and Triage Use Cases

Lower-risk but valuable AI uses
Documentation, patient communication, and triage tools deliver efficiency gains with lower clinical risk.

AI-assisted clinical documentation
Draft notes, summaries, and letters to reduce admin burden and save time.

Patient communication support
Generate clear, personalised explanations and follow-up instructions patients can understand.

Triage support and prioritisation
Assess symptoms and risk levels to help prioritise care and route patients appropriately.

Governance patterns are essential
Clear policies, oversight, and auditability ensure appropriate, ethical, and compliant use.

Safe deployment patterns
Require clinician sign-off, maintain version control, and disclose AI use to patients transparently.

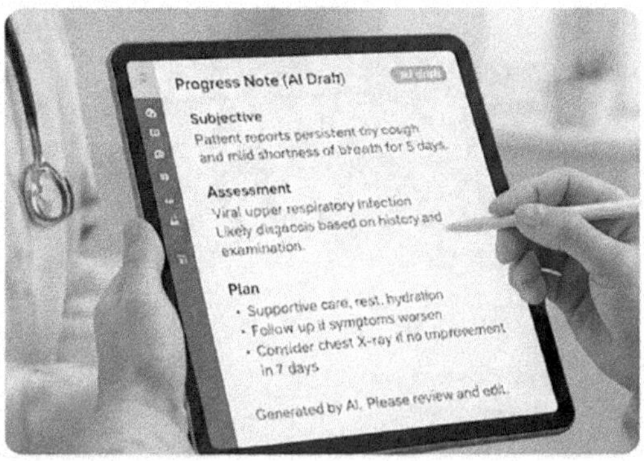

What you Need to Remember

Documentation, patient communication, and triage tools are lower-risk use cases that can deliver significant efficiency and experience benefits—provided they are governed proportionately.

Apply clear policies, human oversight, and transparency to protect patients and build trust. Always disclose AI use, require clinician sign-off, maintain version control, and monitor performance.

The goal is safe, effective support for clinicians—not replacement—enabling better care and smarter workflows.

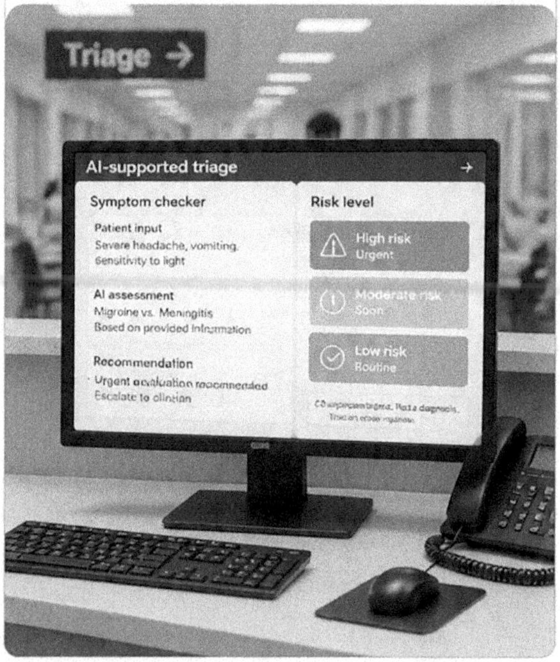

Always require human sign-off	Disclose AI to patients	Escalate edge cases and errors

Section 7: Sector-Specific AI Governance Applications

7.1 Healthcare and Life Sciences

Human Review in High-Stakes Environments

Clinical accountability stays with qualified human.
Accountability for outcomes cannot be delegated to AI.

Even accurate AI can make catastrophic errors.
False positives, data shifts, and rare cases can still cause serious harm.

Human-in-the-loop is the default for clinical AI.
AI supports decisions; it does not replace clinical judgement.

Review must be substantive, not a rushed tick-box.
Genuine engagement with AI output and context is essential.

Guard against automation bias.
Over-reliance on AI can lead to missed errors and harm.

Governance must define who reviews, when, and override powers.
Roles, responsibilities, and escalation paths must be explicit.

What you Need to Remember

In healthcare, clinical accountability is non-delegable. AI can be a powerful assistant but it cannot own the outcome.

Every AI output used in a clinical decision must be meaningfully reviewed by a qualified professional who considers the full context before acting.

Automation bias is a real risk—time pressure and misplaced trust can lead to missed errors and preventable harm.

Governance must clearly specify who reviews, when review is required, the criteria for approval, and how disagreements are handled.

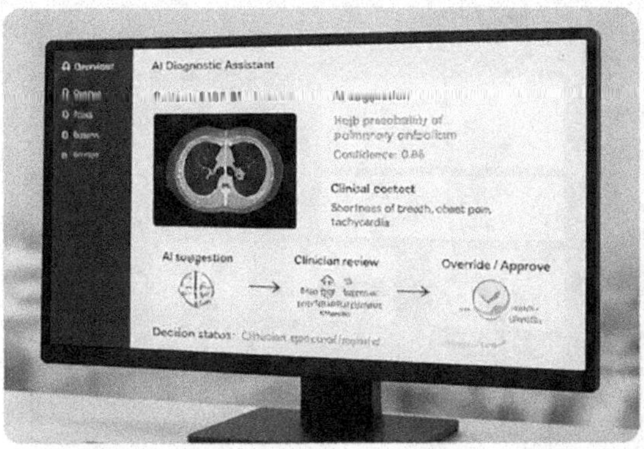

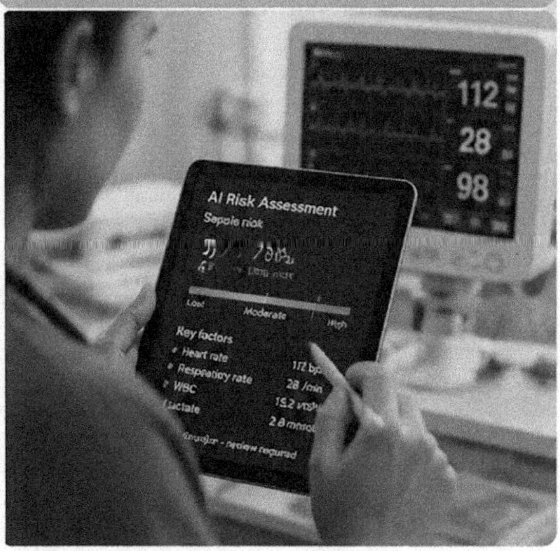

Design reviews for	Build safeguards	Monitor the system
Treatment decisions	time to think	track overrides
Diagnostic reports	access to raw data	investigate disagreements
Triage / prioritisation	easy override button	update training data

Customer-Facing AI in Regulated Contexts

1. **Commercial pressure vs. regulatory duty in financial AI.**

2. Advice, eligibility & customer comms often classed as **high-risk (e.g. EU AI Act).**

3. Eligibility decisions (loans, insurance, products) must be explainable & contestable.

4. Chatbots must not imply personalised regulated advice without authorisation.

5. Customers must be told when AI materially influences a decision.

6. AI-generated comms: tone, accuracy & completeness are compliance issues.

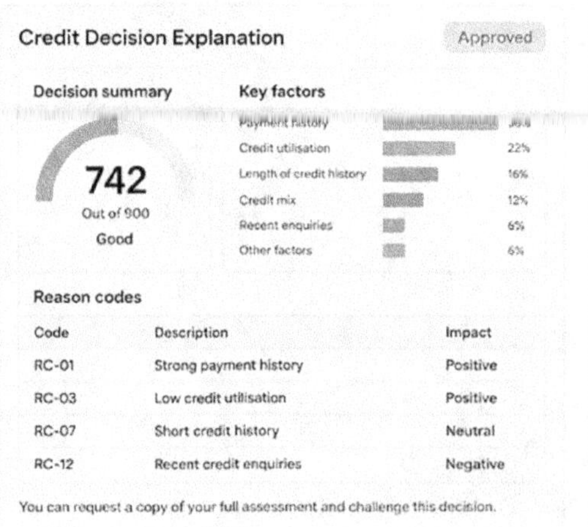

What you Need to Remember

Financial services AI is tightly governed because it affects people's financial wellbeing and rights.

Systems that influence credit, insurance or product access are treated as high-risk and require extra oversight, documentation and transparency.

Automated decisions must be explainable and realistically challengeable by customers.

There is a clear difference between general information chatbots and tools that give personalised financial advice without the right licence.

AI-written emails, statements and policy summaries must go through compliance review because they carry the same obligations as human-written text.

- Check AI is in scope of financial regulations
- Document decision logic & human override paths
- Set up regular compliance review of AI comms
- Provide clear challenge & appeal routes

7.2 Financial Services and Insurance

Spreadsheet AI and Analyst Workflows

1. Excel is core to FS modelling, risk and reporting.
   It remians the backbone of financial analysis and decision-making.

2. AI tools like Microsoft 365 Copilot can write and interpret logic.
   They generate formulas, build models, and explain spreadsheet logic.

3. AI-generated formulas can be subtly wrong and hard to spot.
   Outputs may look plausible but contain logic or reference errors.

4. Treat AI-enhanced spreadsheets as models under MRM frameworks.
   Apply model risk governance just like any other quantitative model.

5. Over-reliance on AI can erode analyst judgement.
   Complacency reduces critical thinking and increases risk of blind spots.

6. Controls: audit trails, change logs, approvals before regulated use.
   Ensure traceability, accountability and appropriate oversight.

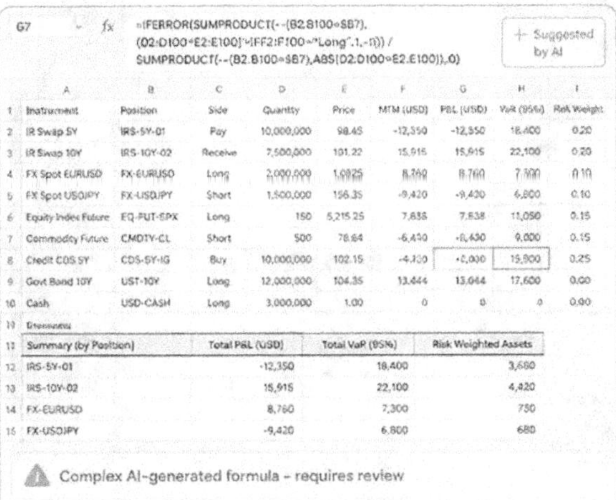

G7 fx =IFERROR(SUMPRODUCT(--(B2:B100=$B7),(D2:D100*E2:E100)*IF(F2:F100="Long",1,-1)) / SUMPRODUCT(--(B2:B100=$B7),ABS(D2:D100*E2:E100)),0)

+ Suggested by AI

	A	B	C	D	E	F	G	H	I
1	Instrument	Position	Side	Quantity	Price	MTM (USD)	P&L (USD)	VaR (95%)	Risk Weight
2	IR Swap 5Y	IRS-5Y-01	Pay	10,000,000	98.45	-12,350	-12,350	18,400	0.20
3	IR Swap 10Y	IRS-10Y-02	Receive	7,500,000	101.22	15,915	15,915	22,100	0.20
4	FX Spot EURUSD	FX-EURUSD	Long	2,000,000	1.0825	8,760	8,760	7,300	0.10
5	FX Spot USDJPY	FX-USDJPY	Short	1,500,000	156.35	-9,420	-9,420	6,800	0.10
6	Equity Index Future	EQ-FUT-SPX	Long	150	5,215.25	7,838	7,838	11,050	0.15
7	Commodity Future	CMDTY-CL	Short	500	78.64	-6,430	-6,430	9,000	0.15
8	Credit CDS 5Y	CDS-5Y-IG	Buy	10,000,000	102.15	-4,130	-6,000	15,900	0.25
9	Govt Bond 10Y	UST-10Y	Long	12,000,000	104.35	13,444	13,044	17,600	0.00
10	Cash	USD-CASH	Long	3,000,000	1.00	0	0	0	0.00
11	[illegible]								

	Summary (by Position)	Total P&L (USD)	Total VaR (95%)	Risk Weighted Assets
12	IRS-5Y-01	-12,350	18,400	3,680
13	IRS-10Y-02	15,915	22,100	4,420
14	FX-EURUSD	8,760	7,300	730
15	FX-USDJPY	-9,420	6,800	680

Complex AI-generated formula - requires review

What you Need to Remember

Excel will remain central to financial services modelling, risk management and reporting.

AI tools are changing how spreadsheet logic is created and interpreted, making analysts far more productive.

AI-generated formulas can look plausible but still be wrong—errors can ripple through models, reports and decisions.

Apply normal model risk governance: assign a clear owner, document reviews and testing, and maintain a complete change log.

Guard against analyst complacency—people tend to trust outputs too easily. Strong governance must catch this drift.

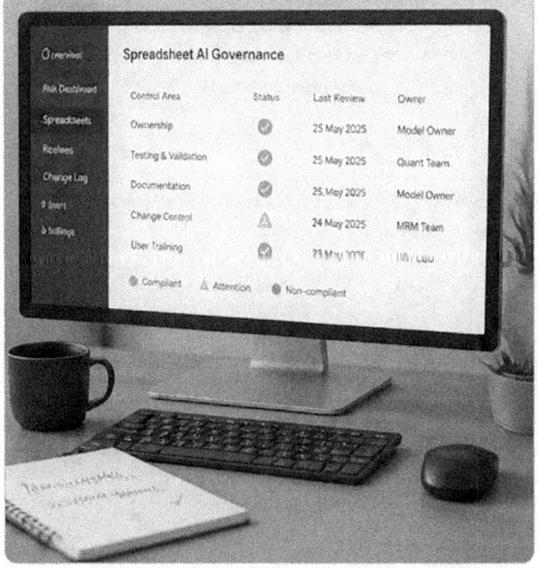

- Escalate material model changes
- Re-test when prompts or data sources change
- Log AI-assisted edits for key spreadsheets
- Schedule periodic human challenge sessions

Fraud, Surveillance, and False Positives

- AI screens payments, claims, identity checks for fraud at scale.
- High-sensitivity models catch more fraud but raise false positives.
- False positives can lock out legitimate customers — often hitting vulnerable groups harder.
- Always-on monitoring of behaviour creates privacy and proportionality risks.
- Fairness tests must compare detection and block rates across demographic groups.
- Human review, appeal routes, and fast fixes are core governance controls.

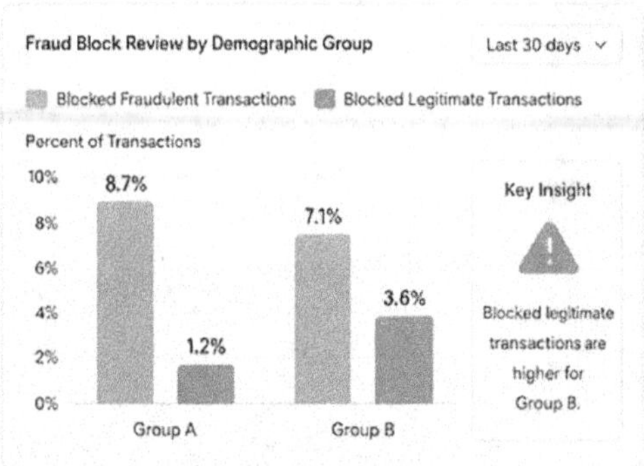

Fairness review of fraud blocks by group.

What you Need to Remember

Fraud AI adds real value — stopping scams, fake claims, and account takeovers at scale. But every model balances recall against false positives.

When certain groups are flagged and blocked more often, a technical setting becomes a fairness, privacy, and compliance issue.

Governance means testing for differential error rates, limiting intrusive surveillance, and making sure people can fix mistakes quickly through usable review and appeal routes.

- Balance fraud loss reduction against customer harm.
- Monitor model performance by segment, not just in aggregate.
- Design clear communications, appeals, and human oversight into every fraud journey.

7.2 Financial Services and Insurance

Auditability for Regulated Decisions

- Make every regulated AI decision documentable, reviewable, and defensible.
- Capture what data went in and why the model or rules produced an output.
- Avoid unexplained black-box models for credit, insurance, and complaints.
- Log model version, inputs, output, and all human review or overrides.
- Ensure customers can challenge a decision by reconstructing what happened.
- Design auditability into systems upfront – retrofits are costly and partial.

AI Decision Audit Trail

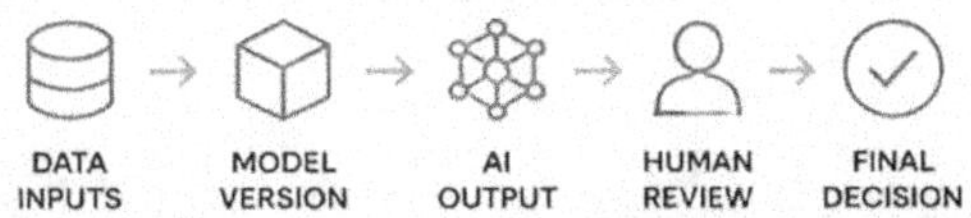

What you Need to Remember

Auditability turns AI governance into something you can prove. For every high-stakes decision, you should be able to show what information the AI used, what it produced, and how a human confirmed or changed it.

That evidence must be captured at the moment of decision, not pieced together later from scattered logs.

When buying or building AI, treat auditability as a core requirement, and avoid black-box models that cannot provide a clear rationale or be wrapped in an explainable layer.

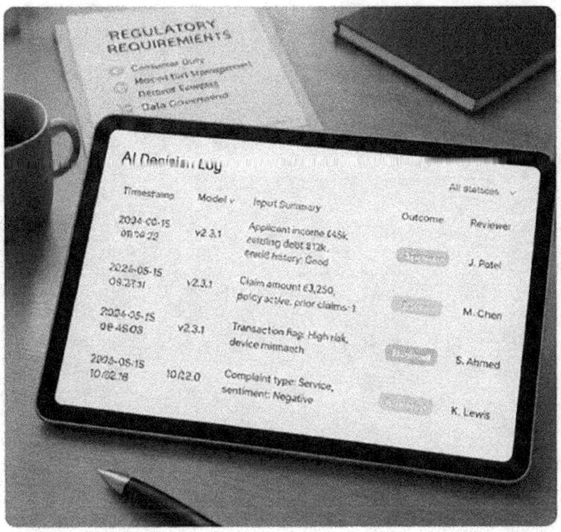

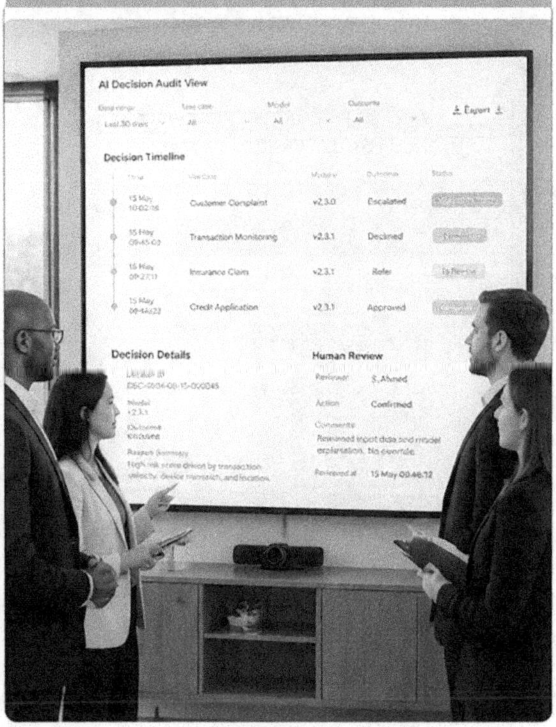

Before launch: define audit requirements and acceptance tests for every AI use case.

During operation: monitor decision logs for bias, errors, and gaps in data capture.

When challenged: retrieve a complete, end-to-end trail within regulatory timeframes.

Section 7: Sector-Specific AI Governance Applications

7.3 Public Sector and Education

AI in Public Services

- Higher accountability standard than commercial AI — public decisions answer to citizens and law.
- Decisions must be transparent, lawful, and open to challenge or appeal.
- AI procurement follows strict rules: fair competition, documentation, and public scrutiny.
- Explainability is mandatory — people have a right to understand automated decisions.
- Legitimacy comes from democratic oversight, not just technical accuracy.
- Weak governance in public AI can erode trust in institutions at scale.

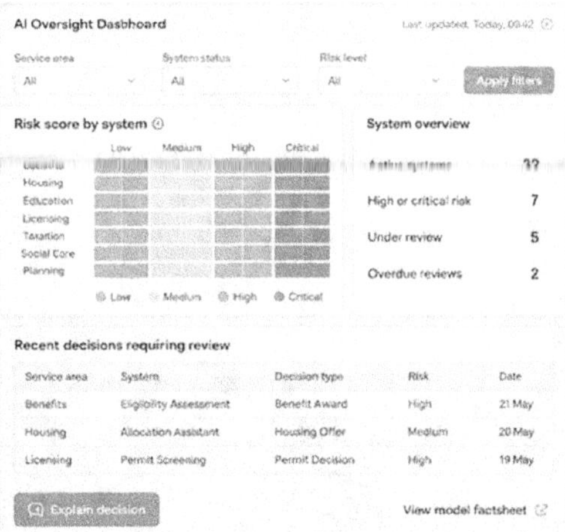

What you Need to Remember

When governments use AI, it isn't just a product choice — it's the exercise of public power. Systems deciding on benefits, permits, or school places must show how they reached ain outcome and be able to withstand legal and democratic challenge.

Procurement should document why AI is used, how suppliers were chosen, and how risks are monitored over time.

Accuracy alone doesn't create legitimacy; citizens need clear routes to question, appeal, and see that elected bodies remain in control.

Because failures in public AI damage trust in whole institutions, governance frameworks need to be especially robust, regularly reviewed, and open to scrutiny.

Explain this decision in plain language for a citizen letter.	List the data sources and checks used before making this recommendation.	Highlight where human approval is required in this workflow.	Suggest risks or groups who might be unfairly impacted.	Draft questions a review board should ask before deployment.

Surveillance, Profiling, and Citizen Rights

- AI surveillance directly impacts privacy and civil liberties.
- Automated profiling can lock historical bias into decisions.
- Facial recognition and predictive policing are among the highest-risk uses.
- Laws like the EU AI Act now treat many of these systems as high-risk or banned.
- People need clear rights to access, challenge, and appeal automated decisions.
- Governance should follow proportionality – use the least intrusive tool that works.

Rights Journey

Person	Data Profile	Decision	Appeal / Remedy
You are observed or assessed	Your data is collected and analysed	An automated decision is made	You can challenge, appeal, and seek redress

What you Need to Remember

AI surveillance and profiling in the public sector are high-stakes. They can shape access to services, freedom of movement, and even safety—often without people realising they are being watched or assessed.

Biased or poor-quality data and predictive policing can unfairly target and disadvantage communities. Automated systems can lock in discrimination at scale if not carefully governed.

Regulations such as the EU AI Act place strict limits on real-time biometric surveillance and other high-risk uses, with some practices prohibited outright.

Citizens must have meaningful ways to know when they've been profiled, contest outcomes, and request human review. Good governance means transparency, accountability, and using the least intrusive, effective option.

When to Escalate AI Surveillance Decisions for Governance Review

- New or expanded surveillance use
- Evidence of biased outcomes
- Use of real-time biometrics
- Cross-agency data sharing
- Public complaints or media scrutiny

AI in Teaching and Assessment

1. Personalised learning & tutoring with AI
AI can adapt content and support to individual student needs.

2. Automated marking & feedback can affect fairness
Algorithms may reflect biased patterns or inconsistent rubrics.

3. AI plagiarism detection can be wrong
False positives can occur and must be reviewed carefully.

4. Protect student data and privacy
Comply with privacy laws and only collect what's necessary.

5. Bias can disadvantage certain student groups
AI systems can perpetuate bias in data, design, or evaluation.

6. Teachers stay responsible; AI only assists
Final decisions, professional judgment, and accountability remain with educators.

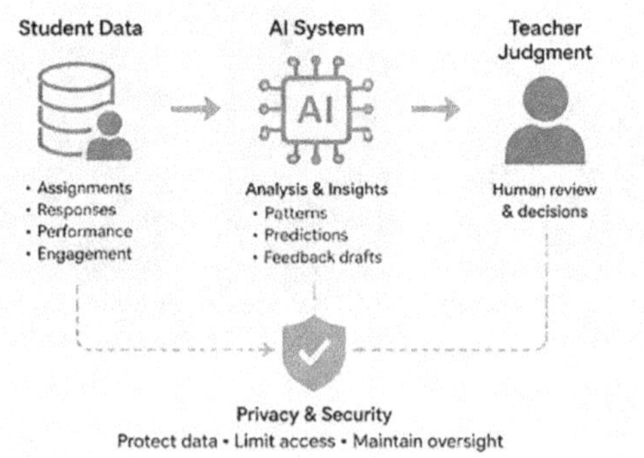

What you Need to Remember

AI can enhance teaching and assessment, but it also introduces important risks that educators must govern carefully.

Fairness and bias require ongoing monitoring to ensure all students are assessed equitably and supported without discrimination.

Student data must be handled lawfully and securely, with transparency about what is collected, how it's used, and who can access it.

AI plagiarism tools can produce false positives, so educator review and context are essential before taking action.

Educators remain accountable for decisions. AI can inform and assist—but human judgment, empathy, and professional responsibility must lead the way.

- Check fairness & bias before rollout
- Explain AI use to students & parents
- Have a human-led appeal process

Accessibility and Inclusion in Public-Facing AI

Serve a diverse population

Public-facing AI must be usable by people of all ages, abilities, languages, cultures, and backgrounds.

Address digital exclusion

Not everyone has reliable internet, modern devices, or high digital literacy. Design for low-bandwidth and low-literacy users.

Meet accessibility standards

Follow WCAG 2.2 AA and relevant disability laws to ensure legally compliant and inclusive AI services.

Design for language and cognition

Use plain language, clear structure, simple interactions, and multilingual support to help everyone understand and engage.

Recognize disproportionate barriers

Older adults and people with disabilities face higher risks of exclusion and poor outcomes from inaccessible AI.

Test for equity and real-world use

Involve diverse users in research and testing to uncover barriers, bias, and usability issues—and act on what you learn.

What you Need to Remember

Public bodies have a legal and moral duty to serve everyone. Public-facing AI must be accessible, inclusive, and fair—so all citizens can understand, access, and benefit from digital services.

AI portals that assume perfect connectivity, modern devices, or high digital literacy risk deepening digital exclusion and creating inequitable outcomes for those who need support most.

Strong governance includes inclusive procurement, accessibility-by-design, regular design reviews, and testing with diverse users to ensure AI services are trusted, usable, and equitable by all.

- Design checklist: WCAG + plain language
- Test with digitally excluded users
- Monitor complaints & drop-off data

ChatGPT, Claude, and Copilot in Staff Workflows

Distinct risk & capability profiles
Each tool has different strengths, limitations, and data handling risks.

ChatGPT for open research & drafting
Best for general research, idea generation, and first drafts using external data.

Claude for deep reasoning & analysis
Ideal for long-document comprehension, policy review, and contract analysis.

Copilot embedded in Microsoft 365
Powerful for productivity inside Microsoft 365, but carries higher internal data exposure risk.

Use an approved tool list
Map each use case to the right tool and required data classification.

Avoid "shadow AI"
Unapproved tools can create security, compliance, and reputational risk.

Approved Tool Register (Example)

Task	Tool	Data Level		
		Public	Internal	Confidential
Client email draft	ChatGPT	✓	✓	
Contract review	Claude		✓	✓
Board paper summary	Copilot		✓	✓

What you Need to Remember

Choosing which AI tool to use is a governance decision, not just a convenience choice. The right tool for the right task—paired with the right data controls—protects your organisation and improves outcomes.

ChatGPT, Claude, and Copilot differ in architecture, data handling, and integration depth. Understanding these differences helps you match the tool to the task and the data classification.

Maintain an approved tool register that maps use cases to tools and data levels. Actively manage "shadow AI" risk through education, clear policies, and monitoring.

Use the Right Tool When...

- Working with sensitive data
- Reviewing long documents
- Drafting client comms
- Automating meeting follow-ups

7.4 Corporate Knowledge Work and Professional Services

AI for Research, Drafting, and Client Materials

Speed with verification
Use AI to draft faster, but verify key facts, numbers, and logic before sharing.

Watch for hallucinations
Be extra cautious when AI cites sources, recalls specific facts, or summarises third-party material.

Higher bar for clients
Client-facing outputs need fuller review than internal notes or early drafts.

Tiered review model
Draft → Internal review → Client sign-off
Light checks for working drafts, mandatory human sign-off for client deliverables.

Track AI involvement
Use version control and audit trails to show where AI assisted in producing significant documents.

Update QC processes
Make sure quality checks explicitly cover AI-generated text as well as human writing.

Documents

Name	Type	Owner	Modified	AI-assisted
Market Analysis Draft.docx	Document	J. Smith	May 13, 2025	Yes
Client Briefing Note.docx	Document	A. Patel	May 12, 2025	Yes
Research Summary.pdf	PDF	M. Chen	May 11, 2025	No
Engagement Proposal.docx	Document	R. Jones	May 9, 2025	Yes
Financial Model.xlsx	Spreadsheet	T. Brown	May 8, 2025	No
Board Presentation.pptx	Presentation	A. Patel	May 6, 2025	Yes
Internal Notes.docx	Document	J. Smith	May 5, 2025	No

What you Need to Remember

AI is now a routine tool for research and drafting in professional services, but professional standards still apply.

Emphasise the tension between speed and verification, calling out hallucinated citations and invented sources as a major risk if users don't check.

A tiered review model, clear version control, and updated quality control keep productivity gains while meeting client and regulatory expectations.

Always verify sources | Protect client trust | Use tiered review | Speed, not shortcuts

Knowledge Management with Agents and Connectors

AI expands access – and risk
Agents can retrieve, summarise, and act on internal knowledge – boosting productivity but widening exposure.

Connectors inherit your access
Linking Copilot or other agents to SharePoint, email, or CRM gives them the same permissions as the authorising user.

Over-permissioned agents leak data
Broad access can surface confidential files, client data, or restricted documents in responses.

Apply least privilege
Give each agent only the data it needs for its defined task or workflow.

Audit connectors regularly
Review which agents can reach which data stores and remove unnecessary access.

Be careful with 'search everything'
Wide-scope prompts may pull in information that shouldn't be shared externally or even across teams.

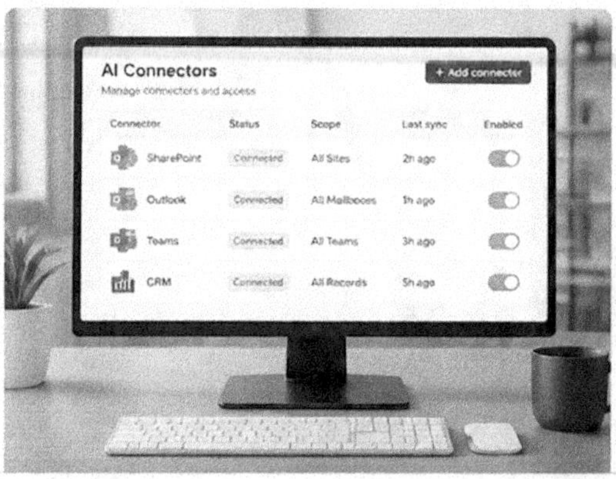

What you Need to Remember

Connecting AI agents to internal systems is powerful but risky: the agent effectively sees whatever the configuring user can see.

The danger is unintended exposure – a simple request like 'summarise everything we know about this client' can aggregate sensitive documents or breach data handling rules.

Design agents with least-privilege access, schedule regular permission reviews, and train staff to use focused prompts instead of open-ended 'search everything' instructions.

Define agent purpose before granting access.

Limit each connector to the minimum data it needs.

Schedule regular audits and staff training on safe prompts.

Billing, Accountability, and Client Transparency

Clarify how AI affects time, fees and scope
Explain when AI reduces or increases effort, how it impacts deliverables, and how you price the work.

Keep practitioner accountability: you sign off, you own the work
AI supports your work, but you remain professionally responsible for results.

Explain AI use in engagement letters, invoices and status updates
Be clear and consistent about where AI contributes to the engagement.

Be ready with a consistent answer when clients ask about AI
Prepare a short, plain-language response that reflects your policy and values.

Define disclosure thresholds by service line and regulator expectations
Disclose when material to the engagement or required by law or professional rules.

Review policies as regulations and norms evolve
Keep your policies current with legal, professional, and client expectations.

Policy-aligned billing view — Export

All Clients | All Matters | May 1 – May 31, 2025

Client	Matter	Service	Date	Hours	Billed	AI-Assisted?
Acme Industries	Corporate Restructure	Analysis	May 12	3.2	$1,120	On
Northbridge Corp.	M&A Due Diligence	Research	May 13	2.5	$875	On
Riverview Partners	Tax Advisory	Drafting	May 14	4.0	$1,400	On
Harbor Health	Regulatory Review	Review	May 15	1.8	$630	Off
Summit Logistics	Contract Negotiation	Drafting	May 16	2.7	$945	On
Bluefield Capital	Investment Memo	Analysis	May 16	1.5	$525	Off

ⓘ AI-Assisted? indicates tasks where AI tools contributed to the work.

What you Need to Remember

Clients pay for professional judgement and outcomes. Traditional billing rules assume human effort—AI changes the effort profile but not the expectation that you deliver quality, compliant work.

Clients will ask about AI use and disclosure. Clear, consistent communication builds trust and sets the right expectations.

Reputational and regulatory risks are real. Inconsistent billing or undisclosed AI use can damage relationships and trigger scrutiny.

The core principle is simple: AI may assist, but responsibility stays with the professional. Be transparent, document your approach, and stand behind your work.

Put it in writing
Standard AI clauses in engagement letters.

Align teams
Train partners and staff on your disclosure position.

Audit regularly
Sample files to check billing and AI use match policy.

SECTION 8

Implementation, Maturity, and Future Readiness

In this section, we look at how organisations put governance into practice, measure maturity and stay ready for a fast-moving future, bringing the course together into an implementation roadmap. We begin with getting started: an honest current-state assessment and tool inventory (often surprising, because AI spreads before governance catches up), prioritising the highest-impact controls such as an acceptable use policy, data-classification guidance and simple prompting rules, governance maturity models as a shared language, and metrics spanning adoption and control coverage.

We then focus on people and culture: role-based AI literacy rather than one course for everyone; prompting and review as core workplace skills, since vague outputs get accepted precisely because nothing looks obviously wrong; decision hygiene to counter automation bias, stronger under time pressure; and a culture of challenge and escalation that makes every other control work.

A substantial block covers the frontier of agentic AI: multi-agent orchestration and its accountability gaps, governing teams of AI systems by scoping sub-agent permissions to the minimum, autonomous workflows and delegated authority, and a practical lens on how much action AI should take (reading, writing, or transacting and deciding). The section, and the course, close on future readiness: frontier and multimodal models that can outdate frameworks within months, new patterns added to already-approved tools, continuous policy refresh, and a governance function designed to absorb change rather than resist it.

Section 8: Implementation, Maturity, and Future Readiness

8.1 Building an AI Governance Roadmap

Current-State Assessment

Inventory all AI tools – capture every system in use, including 'unofficial' ones.

Map users and use-cases – who uses which tools, for what workflows.

Track data flows – what data is entering or leaving each AI tool.

Surface unmanaged risk – shadow AI, personal accounts, unapproved plug-ins.

Record policy gaps – where real behaviour doesn't match written rules.

What you Need to Remember

A current-state assessment gives you a clear, honest picture of how AI is being used across your organisation.

By inventorying tools, mapping users and use-cases, and tracking data flows, you uncover hidden risk, shadow AI, and the gap between practice and policy.

This visibility is essential for prioritising risks, closing policy gaps, and building the right controls without slowing innovation.

Most importantly, it establishes the baseline for your AI governance roadmap – so every decision forward is grounded in reality.

Ask: Where is AI already embedded in workflows?

Ask: What data types are at highest risk?

Ask: Which quick wins will reduce risk fastest?

Section 8: Implementation, Maturity, and Future Readiness

8.1 Building an AI Governance Roadmap

Prioritising the Highest-Impact Controls

1. **Start where harm potential is highest** — not all governance gaps carry equal risk.

2. **Quick wins:** acceptable use policy, data classification guidance, basic prompt rules.

3. **Strategic investments:** review workflows, incident processes, vendor assessments.

4. **Match control intensity to use-case risk** — avoid over-engineering low-stakes scenarios.

5. **Sequence controls** so each layer reinforces the next, rather than isolated fixes.

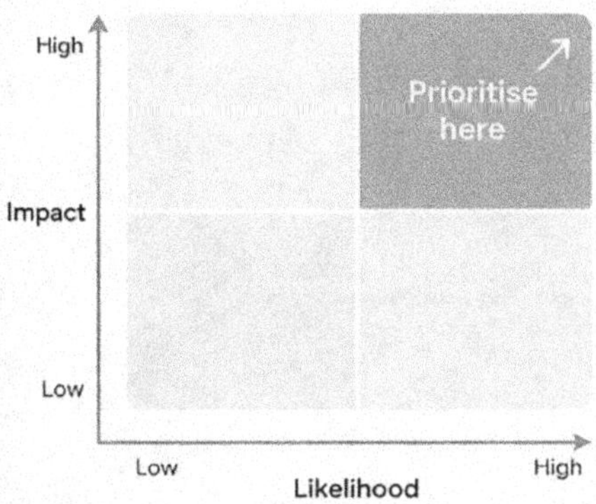

Strong AI governance starts by focusing on the areas where things could go most wrong. Not every gap carries the same risk — concentrate your effort where the potential impact and likelihood are highest.

Set quick wins in place early, such as clear usage rules, data guidance and basic prompt practices. Then invest in the foundations that reduce risk at scale: workflow reviews, incident handling and vendor oversight.

Apply the right level of control for the level of risk. Avoid over-engineering low-risk uses, and sequence controls so each layer builds on the last and strengthens the next.

AI Use Cases

Use Case	Risk Level	Control Focus
Chatbot FAQs	Low	Basic prompts
Document summarisation	Medium	Data controls
AI-assisted credit decisions	High	Full review

What you Need to Remember

- Focus on the highest-risk gaps first.
- Implement quick wins early.
- Invest in review, vendor and incident processes.
- Keep controls proportional to use-case risk and build them in sequence.

Ask: What could go wrong if this AI fails?

Classify the data before you plug it into AI.

Document which controls apply to each use case.

Section 8: Implementation, Maturity, and Future Readiness

8.1 Building an AI Governance Roadmap

Governance Maturity Models

Level 1 – Ad hoc
AI in use with no formal policy, controls, or oversight.

Level 2 – Developing
Basic policies exist; some controls in place but inconsistently applied.

Level 3 – Managed
Defined processes, assigned roles, consistent compliance, and incident tracking.

Level 4 – Optimised
Continuous improvement, metrics-driven governance, and proactive adaptation.

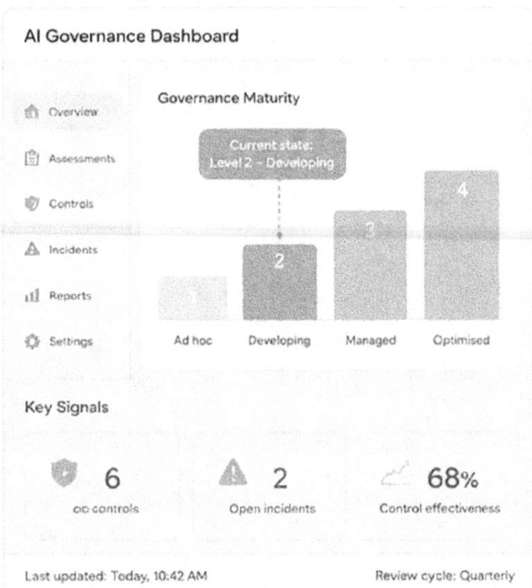

What you Need to Remember

Maturity models give you a shared language and a clear roadmap for strengthening AI governance across your organisation.

They help you explain where you are today and where you're heading tomorrow.

Level 1 means AI is in use with no formal controls—high risk and no accountability.

Level 2 introduces policies and some controls, but they're patchy and inconsistently applied.

Level 3 is where governance starts to work—with defined processes, named owners, consistent compliance, and incident tracking.

Level 4 is self-improving and proactive, using metrics and insights to adapt before issues arise.

The goal isn't getting to the top for its own sake—it's agreeing the right target level for your context and building a realistic plan to get there.

Use the model to...

- Set realistic target level
- Prioritise governance investments
- Track progress for leadership
- Align teams on responsibilities

Section 8: Implementation, Maturity, and Future Readiness

8.1 Building an AI Governance Roadmap

Metrics for Success

Adoption rate
Track active users and use cases to measure responsible AI adoption.

Control coverage
Measure the % of AI systems and processes covered by governance controls.

Incident rate & severity
Monitor AI-related incidents, severity levels, and time to detect and respond.

Trust & confidence indicators
Track stakeholder trust, user satisfaction, and perceived fairness and transparency.

Review cadence
Measure how consistently policies, models, and controls are reviewed and updated.

Risk posture trend
Track risk scores over time to assess improvement and emerging risks.

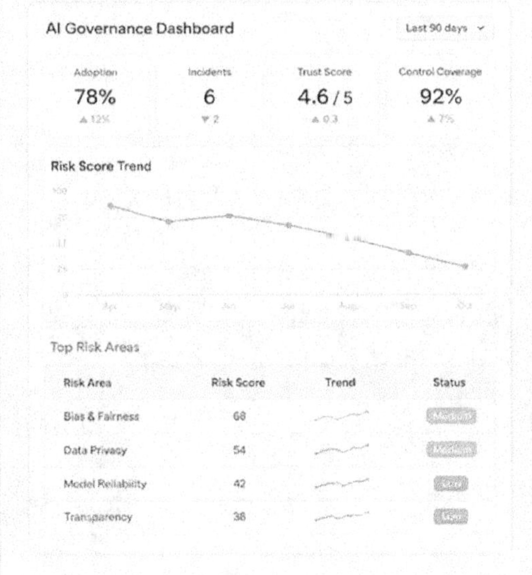

What you Need to Remember

Effective AI governance is measured, not assumed. Focus on the metrics that show whether your controls are working and your organisation is building trust.

Track adoption to understand value realisation, control coverage to ensure protections are in place, and incidents to detect and address issues early.

Monitor trust indicators and risk posture trends to ensure your AI use remains fair, transparent, and aligned with your values and obligations.

Measure today, improve tomorrow, and lead with confidence.

Define KPIs

Build a dashboard

Review regularly

Link to roadmap

8.2 Training and Culture for Responsible AI

Role-Based AI Literacy

Why roles matter

- Different roles interact with AI in different ways and carry different risks.
- One generic AI course rarely works for everyone.

Leaders

- Set direction, risk appetite, and funding for AI controls.
- Need enough literacy to challenge vendor claims and ask the right questions.

Frontline staff

- Use tools like Copilot or chatbots in day-to-day work.
- Need clear rules on approved tools, reviewing outputs, and when to escalate.

Developers & integrators

- Design and connect AI-powered workflows.
- Need depth on model behaviour, prompt risks, and safe system design.

Reviewers & approvers

- Provide meaningful human checks before AI outputs are used.
- Need concrete examples of what 'good review' looks like.

Risk & responsibility by role

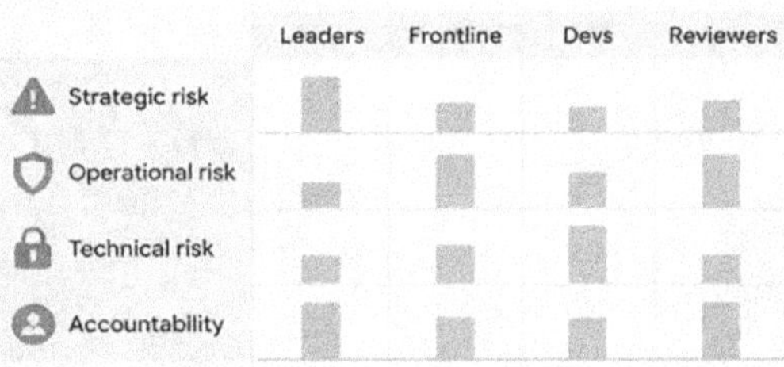

What you Need to Remember

Don't assume the same AI course will work for everyone from the board to the help desk. Roles shape how people use AI and which mistakes actually matter.

Leaders need strategic literacy — enough to set direction, define risk appetite, fund controls, and hold teams accountable, not to master model internals.

Frontline staff need practical, task-level guidance: which tools are approved, how to prompt safely, when outputs look suspicious, and how to escalate issues.

Developers and integrators carry deeper technical risk. Their training should cover prompt injection, tool boundaries, testing, and designing systems that fail safely rather than silently cascading.

Reviewers are often overlooked even though they are the last line of defence. They need clear criteria, examples, and checklists for meaningful human oversight.

Segmenting AI training by role turns a tick-box exercise into real behaviour change.

Designing a role-based AI training plan

1. Map roles & AI use-cases →
2. Prioritise risks & decisions →
3. Build tailored modules & update regularly

Prompting and Review as Core Workplace Skills

- Prompt quality drives accuracy, safety, and compliance — not just speed.
- Vague or messy prompts increase hallucinations and make checking harder.
- Strong prompts define role, task, context, constraints, and output format.
- Review is the other half: read AI responses critically, not on autopilot.
- Verify facts, question gaps in context, and watch for confident errors.
- Embedding these habits turns everyday workflows into responsible AI use.

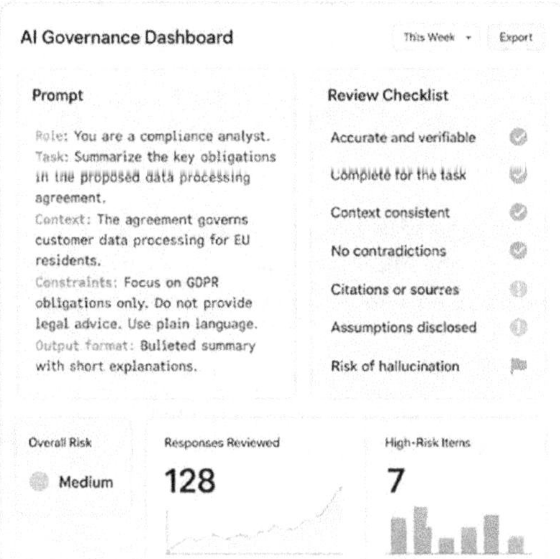

AI can save time and unlock new possibilities, but it only works as well as the prompts we write and the reviews we do.

Clear, structured prompts give AI the right direction. They reduce guesswork, improve accuracy, and produce outputs that are easier to trust and act on.

But even great prompts don't guarantee perfect answers. AI can sound confident while being wrong or incomplete.

That's why review is essential. Read with a critical eye. Check facts, look for gaps, and confirm the reasoning makes sense.

When prompting and review become everyday habits, you build safer workflows, stronger decisions, and more trustworthy AI outcomes.

What you Need to Remember

- Good prompts = clearer, safer outputs.
- Teach people to structure prompts and to doubt polished answers.
- Build a reflex of checking sources, reasoning, and missing pieces.
- The aim is safer, more trustworthy human–AI collaboration.

High-risk decisions	Customer-facing content	Anything using external facts	Mentions of law, finance, or health	Anything you'd sign your name to

Section 8: Implementation, Maturity, and Future Readiness

8.2 Training and Culture for Responsible AI

Decision Hygiene in AI-Assisted Work

Automation bias: over-trusting AI output just because it comes from a system.

Fluent, confident AI text feels persuasive — even for experienced professionals.

Risk for governance: people stop applying their own judgment to consequential decisions.

Decision hygiene = habits that keep human judgment active alongside AI.

Habits: pause before accepting, ask what the AI couldn't know, check independent sources.

Design workflows with mandatory reflection steps — don't rely on willpower alone.

AI suggestion → Human review → Documented decision

What you Need to Remember

Automation bias is subtle and grows with familiarity and convenience.

Experts are just as vulnerable as non-experts.

Overreliance quietly shifts the real decision-maker from human to AI.

Decision hygiene keeps human reasoning engaged: name what the AI couldn't know, identify the assumption most likely to be wrong, pause before approving.

Strongest control = workflow design that forces a short reflection step by default.

Design for double-checks on high-impact decisions.

Record when human judgment overrides or questions AI.

Revisit workflows as systems and policies evolve.

Challenge and Escalation

1. Question AI outputs, especially when they feel 'almost right.'

2. Create psychological safety so challenge is welcomed, not punished.

3. Give clear escalation routes: who to tell, how, and what happens next.

4. Make channels visible and reliable so people believe concerns matter.

5. Leaders model healthy scepticism and act visibly on escalations.

6. Celebrate thoughtful challenge, not just fast compliance.

What you Need to Remember

- Culture makes AI governance work — without safety, training and controls are ignored.
- People must feel that speaking up about doubtful AI outputs is the responsible choice, not a career risk or delay.
- Leaders set the tone by publicly questioning AI results and admitting uncertainty.
- Escalation must be simple and concrete — named channels, shared inboxes, lightweight forms.
- Always close the loop so people see their concerns are acted on.

AI Incident Report

What happened?

Select incident type

Describe the concern

Provide a clear, concise description...

Where did it occur?

System / Tool / Process

Impact (if known)

Select impact level

Additional context (optional)

Add any relevant details...

Submit Concern

- Use AI + human judgement
- Escalate early, not perfectly
- Choose the safest option when in doubt
- Thank people who speak up

Multi-Agent Systems and Orchestration Risk

- Chain of AI agents handling multi-step tasks
- Each agent can act, call tools, pass tasks on
- Responsibility blurs across the chain
- Early errors and bias can quietly snowball
- Govern the whole pipeline as one system
- Control scope, log handoffs, add human checks

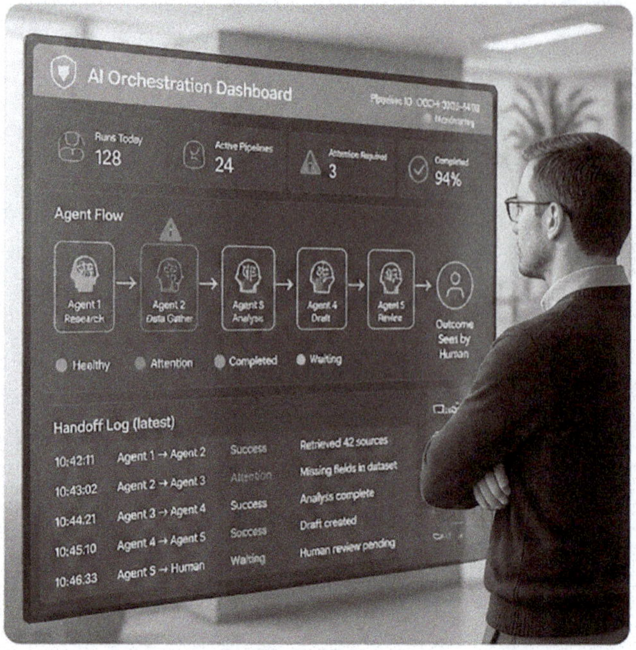

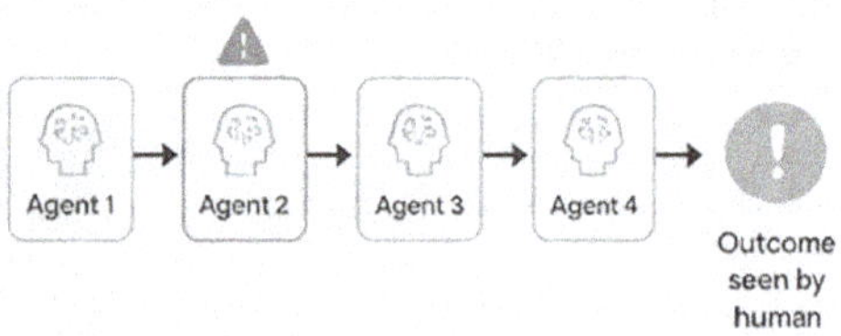

Small early errors can amplify down the chain if no one is watching.

What you Need to Remember

Multi-agent systems are powerful, but they create accountability gaps.

No single agent owns the final result.

Treat orchestration as one accountable system.

Define agent permissions, log every handoff, and insert human review at key decision points, not just at thie end.

- Design clear roles for every agent
- Trace every step in the chain
- Give humans final say on high-impact actions

Governing Teams of AI Systems

- Orchestrator agents direct sub-agents – governance must cover both layers.
- Sub-agents may control tools, files, APIs, or external services.
- Apply least privilege – scope permissions to each agent's role.
- Shared memory and context can leak or contaminate data.
- Design kill switches and circuit breakers at the orchestration level.
- Document each agent's expected behaviour and human escalation triggers.

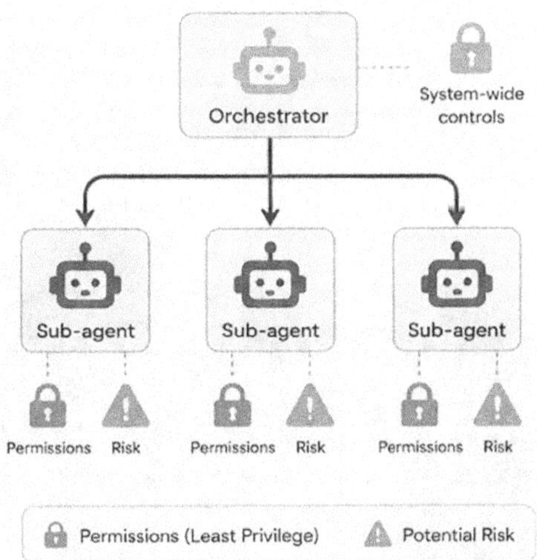

What you Need to Remember

When an orchestrator coordinates multiple agents, governance has to span both tiers.

Give each sub-agent only the access it needs to do its job, especially where files, databases, and external services are involved.

Treat shared context as shared memory – check what data is being passed around and who can see it.

Build a system-wide off switch at the orchestration layer so you can halt a whole workflow cleanly if something behaves unexpectedly.

Underpin everything with clear runbooks that describe what each agent should do and when issues must be handed to a human.

Design
Map every agent, its powers, and its data.

Control
Build least-privilege access and orchestration-level kill switches.

Escalate
Define when humans step in and how to pause the system.

Autonomous Workflows and Delegated Authority

Design AI workflows for multiple steps.
Chain tasks, tools, and decisions while preserving clarity and control.

Delegate along a spectrum.
From AI assist to full automation—match delegation to the task and context.

Match autonomy to stakes.
Higher impact or uncertainty requires more human oversight and checkpoints.

Define clear scope boundaries.
Specify what the AI can do, what it can't, and when to escalate.

Ensure reversibillity.
Every delegated action should be traceable, auditable, and undoable where possible.

Use tiered delegation policies.
Standardize governance with clear tiers and escalation rules.

AI Governance Dashboard

Use case	Risk level	Delegation tier
Invoice processing	Low	AI Execute (High)
Marketing content draft	Low	AI Execute (High)
Customer support reply	Medium	AI Assist + Human Approve
Contract review summary	Medium	AI Assist + Human Approve
Vendor onboarding	High	Human Approve
Pricing change approval	High	Human Approve
Fund transfer request	High	Human Approve + Escalate

Workflow routing (example)

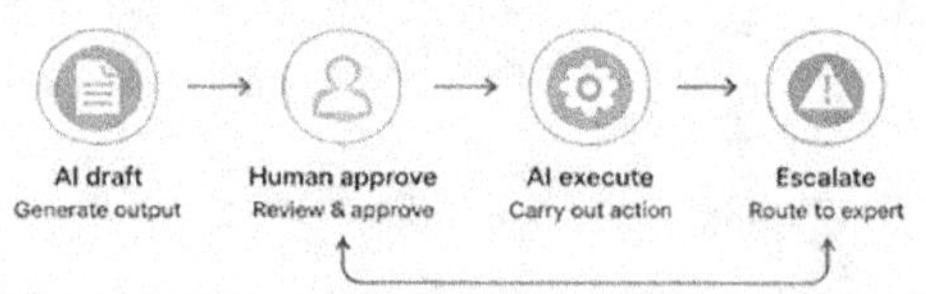

What you Need to Remember

Autonomous workflows only work when delegation is deliberate. Define what the AI can do, when it should act, and when humans must step in.

Match the level of autonomy to the stakes. Higher impact, uncertainty, or regulatory sensitivity means tighter control and more human oversight.

Set clear scope boundaries and escalation triggers so the AI operates within approved limits and flags when it's outside its lane.

Apply the reversibility test: if an action can't be traced, audited, and undone, it shouldn't be delegated.

Use tiered delegation policies to standardize decisions, ensure consistency, and scale responsible automation.

High financial impact

Legal or regulatory risk

Irreversible changes

Customer-facing automation

How Much Action Should AI Be Allowed to Take

Action Types
Read, write, communicate, transact, decide.

Low-Risk: Read
Analyse, summarise, retrieve information only.

Medium-Risk: Write & Communicate
Emails sent, documents filed, messages posted.

High-Risk: Transact & Decide
Place orders, grant access, delete or change data.

Govern with Intent
Explicitly permit or restrict each action per use case.

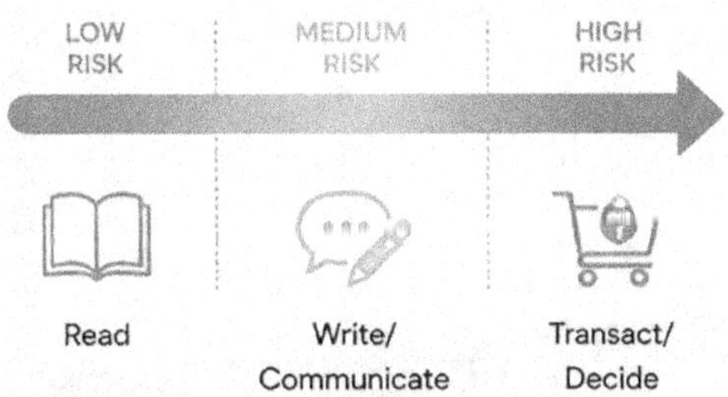

What you Need to Remember

Think about AI by what it can actually do. Reading and summarising information is low risk because nothing in the real world changes. Once AI starts writing or communicating for you, every message has reputational and compliance impact. When it can transact or decide—spend money, change records, grant access—the stakes are highest and tight governance is essential.

For every AI use case, specify which action types are allowed, keep the default restrictive, and only expand permissions when there is a clear, documented reason.

SET SAFE AI ACTION LEVELS

Read: default allowed	Write/Communicate: human review first	Transact: rare, tightly controlled	Decide: only with oversight	Document: who approves which actions

Frontier Models, Multimodal Systems, and Office Agents

Frontier models: fast-evolving reasoning, code, vision, and voice capabilities.

Multimodal: one system can handle text, images, audio, video, and documents together.

Office agents: AI embedded in email, documents, spreadsheets, and chats, acting directly on files and calendars.

Each modality exposes different data risks — e.g. hidden image metadata or personal details in audio.

Text-only governance misses these new risk surfaces.

Update use-case intake to record which modalities are involved, not just the task.

AI Use-case Intake Form

Use-case: Meeting summary agent

Which modalities are involved?

- [x] Text
- [x] Images
- [x] Audio
- [ ] Video
- [x] Documents

Brief description

Summarise meetings, action items, and follow-ups across transcripts and shared documents.

Business owner

Operations Team

What you Need to Remember

Frontier and multimodal models evolve so quickly that text-only governance becomes obsolete in months. Modern systems can read and generate across images, audio, video, and documents, and office agents bring these capabilities straight into tools like email and spreadsheets.

Each format carries different privacy and confidentiality risks, so approvals and policies must ask which modalities are used and how real business data is accessed.

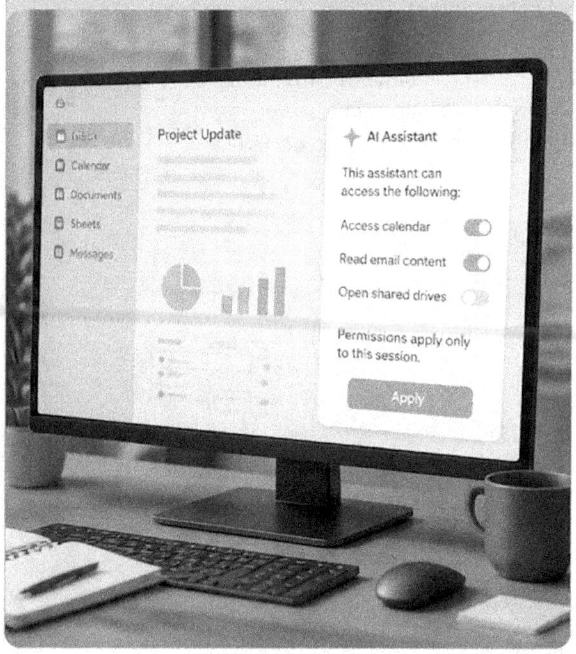

Review governance against new model releases every 3–6 months.

Assess risks by modality: text, files, images, audio, video.

Include data sensitivity and access permissions in every AI use-case intake.

8.3 Future-Proofing Governance for Fast-Moving AI

Anticipating New Operational Patterns

1. AI releases are continuous, not annual.
2. New features can appear inside tools already in use.
3. Governance teams track product changelogs and release notes.
4. Horizon scanning is a named responsibility.
5. Tabletop exercises test near-future AI scenarios.
6. Modular policies are easier to update than monolithic ones.

AI capabilities in familiar tools—like office suites, collaboration platforms, and CRMs—change rapidly and often without major version jumps.

Organizations must monitor product changelogs and release notes continuously to understand new capabilities, default settings, and limitations.

Assign owners for horizon scanning who track upcoming features, assess impact, and escalate material changes to governance.

Run scenario-based tabletop exercises that explore near-future use cases, risks, and control gaps.

Design modular policies mapped to individual capabilities so updates can be made quickly, targetedly, and with clear audit trails.

What you Need to Remember

When to revisit AI policies	Major product update	New agentic or autonomous features	Incidents or near-misses

Continuous Policy Refresh

Static AI policies age fast
Outdated policies create false confidence and increase exposure.

Refresh when new AI tools are adopted
Align policies with how people actually work.

Refresh after regulatory or risk updates
Keep pace with changing laws, standards, and risks.

Hold at least quarterly scheduled reviews
Build review cadences into governance routines.

Give every policy an owner and version number
Ensure accountability and clear audit trails.

Use incident and near-miss data to improve controls
Close gaps and strengthen policies continuously.

Policy Lifecycle

Draft → Approve → Communicate → Review

What you Need to Remember

Effective AI governance depends on continuous policy refresh. Static policies quickly lose relevance as tools, risks, and regulations evolve. Regular reviews ensure controls remain aligned with how AI is actually used.

Assign clear owners, apply version control, and document changes. Track what changed, when, why, and who approved it. This builds auditability and strengthens governance credibility.

Use real-world signal—incidents, near misses, and user feedback—to improve policies and reduce risk. Communicate every update clearly so teams understand what changed and why.

- Set triggers: new tools, new rules, incidents
- Schedule quarterly reviews
- Always communicate what changed and why

Keeping Governance Aligned with Evolving Products and Regulation

- AI products change quickly – governance fills the gap until rules catch up.
- Regulation like the EU AI Act will be clarified via guidance, standards and case law.

- Run a regulatory watch: monitor key authorities and standards bodies.
- Map internal policies and controls directly to external requirements to expose gaps.

- Involve legal, compliance and technology – no single team can track everything.
- Treat AI governance as an ongoing programme with regular review cycles.

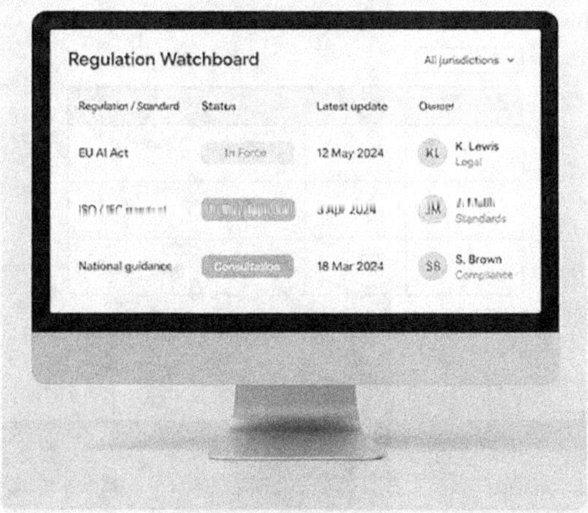

AI governance lives in the space between fast-moving technology and slower-moving regulation. Products, models and data practices evolve week by week, while rules emerge through guidance, standards and case law.

That's why organisations need a regulatory watch and a living map of policies and controls linked to external requirements. This makes gaps visible early and keeps you ready for change.

Governance is not a legal team project.
It requires collaboration across legal, compliance, technology, product and risk so that decisions are practical and aligned with business goals.

Treat AI governance as a continuous improvement loop--with regular reviews, feedback from operations, and updates as new obligations and risks emerge.

What you Need to Remember

- Regulation will keep evolving – design governance to adapt.
- Maintain a living map between policies, controls and external rules.
- Share responsibility: legal, compliance and tech work together.
- Treat AI governance as a continuous improvement loop, not a one-off project.

Useful prompts for your governance team

- Where are our highest AI risks versus current regulation?
- What changed in the last quarter that might affect our controls?

Building a Governance Function That Can Adapt

Establish clear ownership.
Designate an AI governance owner with the mandate, authority, and resources to act.

Run a governance board monthly.
Bring together cross-functional leaders to review risks, decisions, and upcoming changes.

Create frontline feedback channels.
Encourage staff to raise concerns and ideas through simple, safe, and visible channels.

Document decisions and cycles.
Capture policies, decisions, and rationale so the team can learn and stay aligned.

Assume change and build for it.
Design governance to be flexible, so it can adapt as tools, risks, and regulations evolve.

The Adaptive Governance Loop

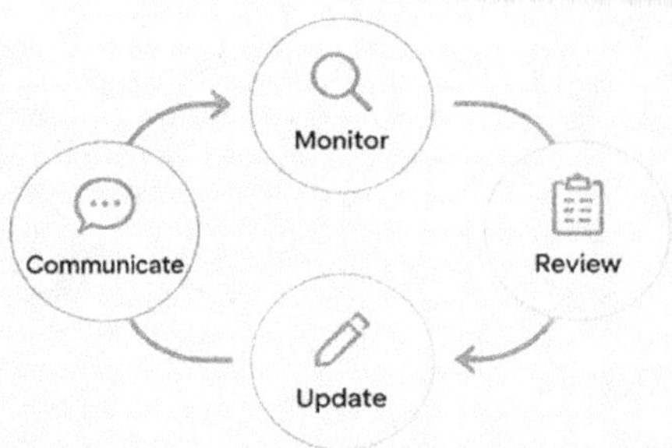

What you Need to Remember

Adaptive governance starts ownership.
Someone must be empowered to make AI governance real in your organization.

Review regularly, not reactively.
A monthly governance board keeps your oversight proactive and consistent.

Listen to the front line.
People closest to the workspot issues first. Give them an easy way to speak up.

Document as you go.
Clear records of decisions and policies create transparency and help you improve over time.

Build for change.
Assume your framework will need to evolve—and make that part of the plan.

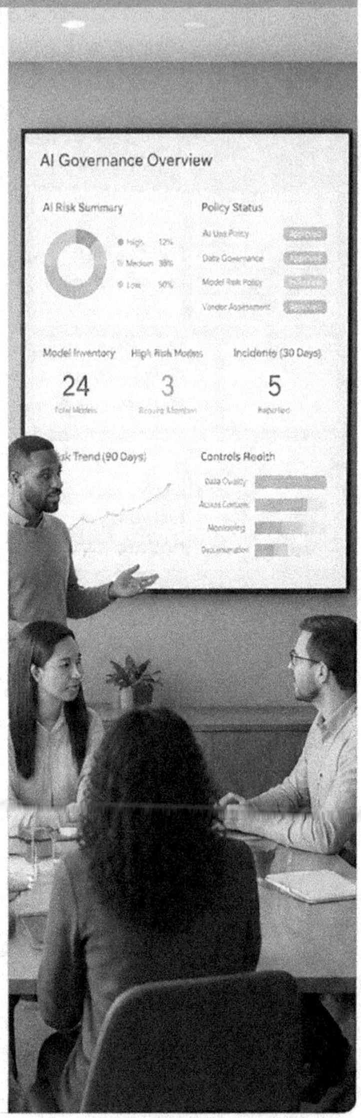

Who owns AI decisions?
Name the owner and confirm their mandate.

How often do we review?
Set a cadence and stick to it—consistency builds confidence.

Where do issues get reported?
Make it easy, safe, and visible for everyone.

More in the AI Visual Reference Series

This is the first title in a growing series, each volume applying the same visual, look-it-up approach to a different professional domain. New titles are added regularly. Search "AI Awareness Visual Reference" or visit www.aiawareness.ai for the complete, up-to-date list.

#	Title
1	AI Governance and Ethics Visual Reference
2	AI in Change Management Visual Reference
3	AI in Risk and Audit Visual Reference
4	AI in Cybersecurity Visual Reference
5	AI in Data Analytics Visual Reference
6	AI in Knowledge Management Visual Reference
7	AI in Research and Development Visual Reference
8	AI in Innovation and Digital Transformation Visual Reference
9	AI in Product Management Visual Reference
10	AI in IT Management Visual Reference
11	AI in Human Resources Visual Reference
12	AI in Learning and Development Visual Reference
13	AI in Executive Leadership Visual Reference
14	AI in Legal and Compliance Visual Reference
15	AI in Marketing Visual Reference
16	AI in Sales Visual Reference
17	AI in Customer Experience Visual Reference
18	AI in Customer Service Visual Reference
19	AI in Finance Visual Reference
20	AI in Sustainability and ESG Reporting Visual Reference
21	AI in Facility Management Visual Reference
22	AI in Supply Chain Management Visual Reference
23	AI in Procurement Visual Reference
24	AI in Project Management Visual Reference
25	AI in Operations Visual Reference
26	AI in Manufacturing Visual Reference

#	Title
27	AI in Construction and Engineering Visual Reference
28	AI in Real Estate Visual Reference
29	AI in Transportation and Logistics Visual Reference
30	AI in Energy and Utilities Visual Reference
31	AI in Telecommunications Visual Reference
32	AI in Agriculture and Food Production Visual Reference
33	AI in Financial Institutions Visual Reference
34	AI in Insurance Visual Reference
35	AI in Healthcare Visual Reference
36	AI in Pharmaceuticals and Life Sciences Visual Reference
37	AI in Public Sector and Government Visual Reference
38	AI in Retail Visual Reference
39	AI in Hospitality Visual Reference
40	AI in Media and Entertainment Visual Reference

www.ingramcontent.com/pod-product-compliance
Lightning Source LLC
LaVergne TN
LVHW082335200926
848481LV00012B/3353
* 9 7 9 8 9 0 1 4 8 9 2 5 3 *